ONE Stroke™

TECHNIQUES GUIDE

TECHNIQUES GUIDE

By Donna Dewberry

So Beautiful • So Easy • So Plaid™

© 2003 Plaid Enterprises, Inc.
Norcross, GA 30091-7600

www.plaidonline.com
800/842-4197   04/03
Printed in U.S.A.

ISBN: 1-55895-059-1

DEDICATION

I would like to dedicate this book to two very important people who devote themselves to the production of all the necessary products that it takes to make these books possible. I can't tell you just how much time and energy they spend in assisting with the development of brushes, paints, videos and all the other assorted items. I know that sometimes I can be pretty demanding, but they always seem to get me back on track and help me to see the reasoning behind many decisions. I appreciate their honesty and the fact that they try to get me to meet my deadlines — even though in many instances the deadlines are almost impossible to meet. These ladies are creative, yet focused and are an inspiration to me because of the manner in which they handle their responsibilities. I appreciate all they do and don't express that to them enough. So Dede and Jennifer, "Thank you!"

About Donna Dewberry

Donna Dewberry has been involved with arts and crafts all of her married life – over 30 years. After many evenings of painting at her dining room table, she developed a technique for stress-free painting that became the basis for the One Stroke technique and her series of One Stroke painting books.

Donna has kept the vision of the important basic things needed for a happy and successful life – her family, her religion, and her painting. It's true in painting, as well, that there are some very important basic techniques that every painter needs to know for success. Once you learn and practice the basics of the One Stroke technique, you will be able to paint any design in this book.

ACKNOWLEDGEMENTS

When I reflect upon who I would like to acknowledge in my books, I often feel as though I need to acknowledge a great many people. There are so many who have a part in a book's production. As I began this book I reflected upon this fact and came to a clear understanding of my feelings about acknowledging those involved.

I would like to thank everyone who has assisted in any form with this book. Thanks to those who have edited, those who have painted or will paint, thanks to all those who will print, market, stock, ship or handle this book. Thanks to all those suppliers of surfaces, to the photographers and the photo stylists, thanks to all those retailers and distributors who make each book possible. Thanks to all those who may have shared ideas, to all my staff for all their work, to my family for allowing me time to complete this book. Thanks to all those decorative painters who have inspired me and to anyone and everyone who has ever had a dream — because dreams really can come true! Last but most important of all I would like to acknowledge that any and all talents I am blessed with come from God. Thank you.

THE mariadewberry CHILDREN'S FOUNDATION

ONE STROKE CERTIFICATION

For information on Donna's three-day seminar, where you can learn her painting techniques as well as how to start a business in decorative painting and tips for being a good teacher, how to demo in stores, and how to get your painting published, contact her one of these ways:

• *By mail:*
Dewberry Designs
124 Robin Road, Suite 1700
Altamonte Springs, FL 32701

• *By phone:*
407-339-0239

• *By fax:*
407-339-5513

• *On the Web:*
www.onestroke.com (certification and seminar information)
www.thestrokingedge.com (complete ONE Stroke™ resource)

• *By e-mail:*
onestrokefl@earthlink.net

TABLE OF CONTENTS

This book teaches you how to use FolkArt® Paints and the various sizes and types of ONE Stroke™ brushes to create the strokes that make up the beautiful flowers, foliage, and whimsical critters of the ONE Stroke™ painting technique.

You'll learn about what supplies you need and how to use them. Step-by-step photos show you how to load the brushes and paint the strokes. I painted the strokes on numerous worksheets so you can see exactly how they look. (And do feel free to cover them with a piece of plastic and paint right over them for practice.) There are lots of photos of my designs painted on a variety of surfaces that I hope will guide and inspire you, plus information on preparing surfaces, using painting mediums, and finishing.

Once you've learned how to load the brush and have mastered the various strokes, you can paint any design in this book – from a single flower to an entire bouquet. Enjoy!

ONE STROKE™ SUPPLIES

Using the proper paints and tools will help you achieve success with the One Stroke technique. On these two pages, I've included information about the paints and painting mediums I use.

FolkArt® Paints

FolkArt® Acrylic Colors are high quality bottle acrylic paints. Their rich and creamy formulation and long open time make them perfect for decorative painting. They are offered in a huge range of wonderful, pre-mixed colors and in gleaming metallic shades. Because FolkArt® paints are acrylic-based, cleanup is easy with soap and water.

FolkArt® Artists' Pigments™ are pure colors that are perfect for mixing your own shades. Their intense colors and creamy consistency are wonderful for blending, shading, and highlighting.

FolkArt® Sparkles™ are paints that add subtle iridescence or bright shimmer. They are available in a variety of bright and subtle colors.

FolkArt® Floating Medium

I use **Floating Medium** (868) to help the paint stay wetter for shading and to create transparent paint effects. But please, **don't** follow the instructions on the bottle when using Floating Medium with the One Stroke Technique – if you do, your strokes will be muddy. See the General Instructions for how Floating Medium should be used.

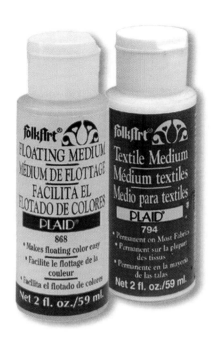

FolkArt Textile Medium

I use **Textile Medium** (794) with FolkArt Acrylic Colors and FolkArt Artists' Pigments to paint permanent, washable designs on fabric. This medium helps acrylic paint absorb into fabric better.

FolkArt Enamels™

FolkArt Enamels have a highly pigmented acrylic polymer formulation with excellent hiding qualities. This line is available in a wide palette of all my beautiful colors chosen from the FolkArt paint collection.

FolkArt Enamels can be mixed, blended, and brushed like other FolkArt paints, and they have the same names as their FolkArt Acrylic Color counterparts.

FolkArt Enamels are waterbase and non-toxic and dry to an opaque finish and gloss sheen. Cleanup (while wet) is easy with soap and water. Best of all, glass and ceramic pieces painted with FolkArt Enamels can be handwashed and are top-rack dishwasher safe once cured.

Paint for Plastic

Plaid's Paint For Plastic makes it easy to use my One Stroke painting technique to decorate and embellish a wide variety of hard plastic items – vases, serving pieces, tableware, ornaments, storage cubes and boxes, and even insulated coolers! You can use it on flexible (soft) plastic items as well – simply undercoat the design with Paint for Plastic Primer (1396) before painting your design. For extra durability, coat your painted area with the Paint for Plastic Sealer (1398).

11

Reusable Teaching Guides

Use these unique laminated worksheets to practice your strokes. To learn and practice, paint right on top of the illustrations and follow the strokes, then wipe clean and paint again! The *blank* Reusable Teaching Guide is a great way to practice once you've mastered the strokes with the illustrated guides.

You can also lay plastic sheets over the worksheets in this book and practice the strokes on the sheets.

FolkArt® Finishes

Apply finish to your painted projects to protect your beautiful painting and add sheen to the surface. I like clear, non-yellowing spray sealers best.

FolkArt® Sanding Sealer (772) seals all pores in wood and creates a velvety finish on raw wood.

FolkArt® Lacquers are a good choice for final finishing. I use lacquer sealers on items that will be used outdoors – they dry very hard, provide good protection from the weather, and won't yellow in the sun and weather like most other sealers. FolkArt Lacquers come in three finishes: **Matte** (773), **Satin** (774), and **Gloss** (775).

FolkArt® Artists' Varnish: can be used on wood and other porous surfaces when a brush-on waterbase varnish is desired. Artist's Varnish is available in gloss, satin, and matte sheens.

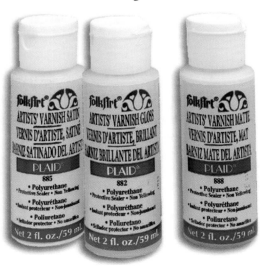

Miscellaneous Supplies

One Stroke Paint Wipes (6023) can be used to clean wet or dry paint from teaching guides.

One Stroke Double Loader (1002) is a tool that you attach to your palette to aid in the double loading technique.

Tracing paper, for tracing patterns from pattern sheets.

Transfer paper and **stylus,** for transferring patterns.

Brush Plus® Brush Cleaner 20480, for cleaning brushes

Paper towels, for blotting brushes. ❑

Sponge Painting Tools

■ ONE STROKE™ SPONGE PAINTERS

One Stroke Sponge Painters (1195) is a set of two sponges that work well for stenciling, painting large surfaces, or creating interesting background effects.

■ KITCHEN SPONGE

A kitchen cellulose or household sponge – the kind you can buy at the grocery store – can be used for applying paint to large surfaces or creating backgrounds.

■ PAINT ROLLER

A foam roller is a handy way to apply a basecoat.

■ WALL FAUX SPONGE

For painting really large items or surfaces such as walls, this large sponge is the perfect tool.

Pictured clockwise from center top: Wall Faux Sponge, kitchen sponge, One Stroke Sponge Painters, foam roller

ONE Stroke™ Palette

The One Stroke Palette (1001) is an easy-to-hold, durable accessory that keeps paint and tools at your fingertips. There are numerous paint wells and spaces for brushes and a paper towel. It can be used by right- or left-handed painters.

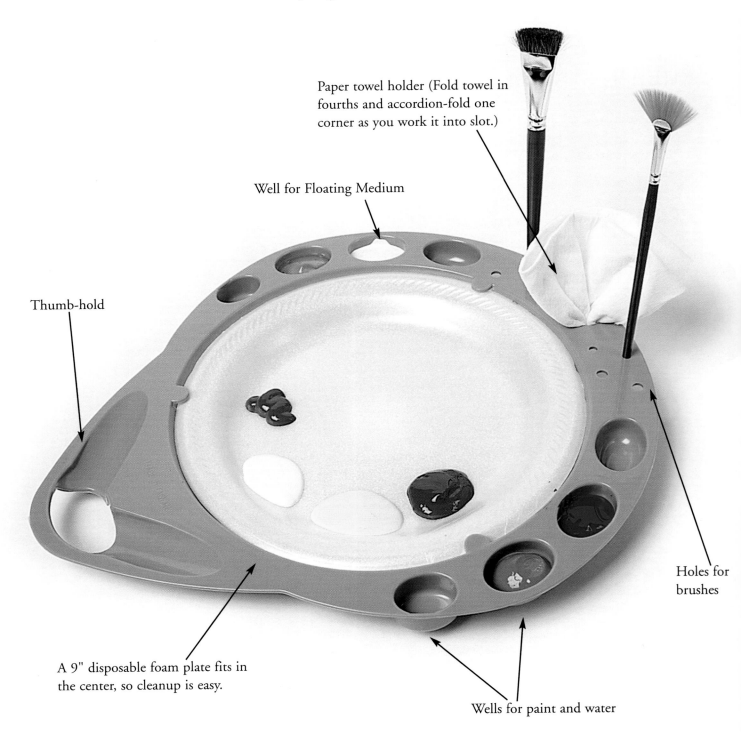

Paper towel holder (Fold towel in fourths and accordion-fold one corner as you work it into slot.)

Well for Floating Medium

Thumb-hold

Holes for brushes

A 9" disposable foam plate fits in the center, so cleanup is easy.

Wells for paint and water

ONE Stroke™ Brush Caddy

The Brush Caddy (1060) is made for rinsing brushes, but it's also a multi-functional box for drying and storing brushes and toting paints and supplies.

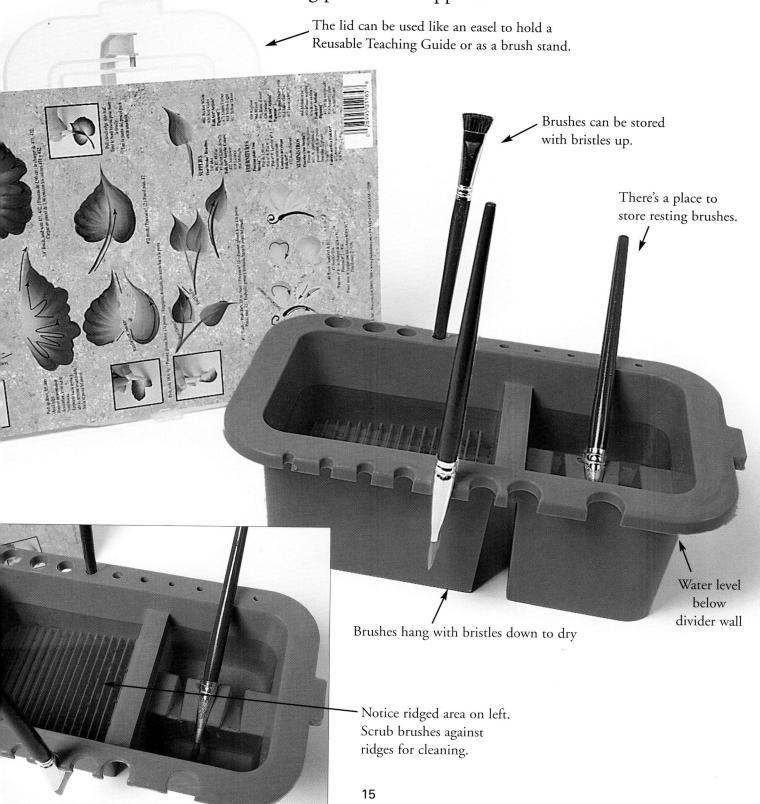

The lid can be used like an easel to hold a Reusable Teaching Guide or as a brush stand.

Brushes can be stored with bristles up.

There's a place to store resting brushes.

Water level below divider wall

Brushes hang with bristles down to dry

Notice ridged area on left. Scrub brushes against ridges for cleaning.

ONE Stroke™ Brushes

Each brush has a specific use. Later in this book you will see how to use and what to paint with each brush.

■ FLAT BRUSHES

One Stroke flat brushes are designed with longer bristles and less thickness in the body of the brush bristles than other flat brushes, so they have a much sharper chisel edge. A sharp chisel edge is essential as most strokes begin and end on the chisel edge.

Remember everyone's comfort zone is different. While one painter is comfortable using a #10, another painter may be just as comfortable with a 3/4" flat brush. Use the size brush that is suitable for the size of your project and with which you feel most comfortable.

Flat brushes are available in the following sizes:
#2 flat (1273)
#6 flat (1274)
#8 flat (1275)
#10 flat (1276)
#12 flat (1058)
#16 flat (1204)
3/4" flat (1176)
1" flat (1184)
1-1/2" (1189)

■ LINERS

The #1 script liner (sometimes referred to as the mini) is used for small detail work where a lot of control is needed. The #2 script liner is used where less control is needed, such as when painting curlicues or string ribbons. They are used with paint that is inky (thinned with water to the consistency of ink). Clean script liners as you would flats; be gentle, but clean thoroughly.

#1 script liner (1271)
#2 script liner (1272)

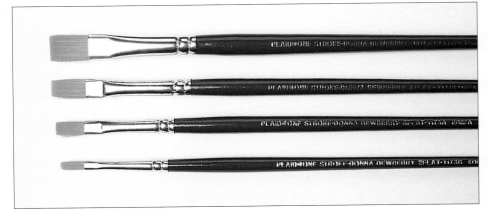

■ SCRUFFY BRUSHES

I originally created the scruffy by shaping the bristles of an old, worn out brush into an oval after carefully cutting them to a uniform length of about 1/2". The One Stroke scruffy brushes you can buy are ready to use. All you have to do is "fluff the scruff" – remove the brush from the packaging and form the bristles into an oval shape by gently pulling them, then twist the bristles in the palm of your hand until they are a nice oval shape. Now you're ready to paint.

A fluffed scruffy brush is used to paint mosses, wisteria, lilacs, and some hair and fur, faux finishes, and shading textures. This brush is not used with water. To clean, pounce the bristles in the water reservoir of the Brush Caddy – don't rake them; the natural bristles can break. Allow the brush to dry before painting again.

Scruffy brushes are available in the following sizes:

1/4" Mini scruffy (1174)
1/2" Regular scruffy (1206)
3/4" Medium scruffy (1172)
1" Large scruffy (1190)

■ ANGLE BRUSHES

Angle brushes are similar to flat brushes, but the bristles are cut at an angle. The One Stroke Angle Brush Set (1278) includes 3/8", 5/8", and 3/4" sizes of angle brushes. Use these for comma strokes – they are also helpful for painting center of rose.

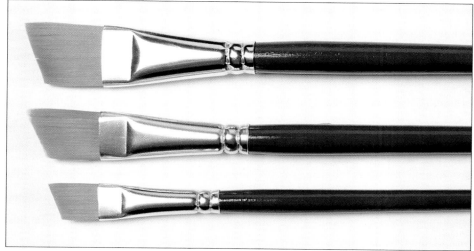

■ FILBERT BRUSHES

Filbert brushes are similar to flat brushes, but they have slightly rounded tips. The One Stroke Filbert Brush Set (1205) includes #6, #8, and #10 filbert brushes. These are helpful for painting petal flowers.

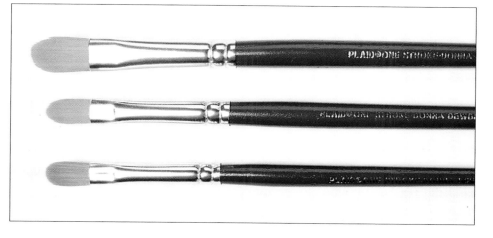

■ FAN BRUSHES

Fan brushes area specialty brushes that I use for painting fur and grass. They are available in the following sizes:

Large #4 fan (1196)
Small #2 fan (1277)

■ ENAMEL BRUSHES

These high-quality brushes were designed especially for use with FolkArt Enamels. Their soft bristles hold paint well and allow paint to glide smoothly on non-porous surfaces, minimizing brush strokes. Wooden handles offer a comfortable grip; metal ferrules hold bristles firmly.

Enamels Basic Brush Set (4150): This set of synthetic bristle brushes includes a 3/4" flat, 1/2" flat, and #2 script liner.

Enamels Mini Brush Set (4151): This set of synthetic bristle brushes includes a #2 flat, #6 flat, and #1 script liner.

Enamels Scruffy Brush (4152): This is a natural bristle 3/4" scruffy.

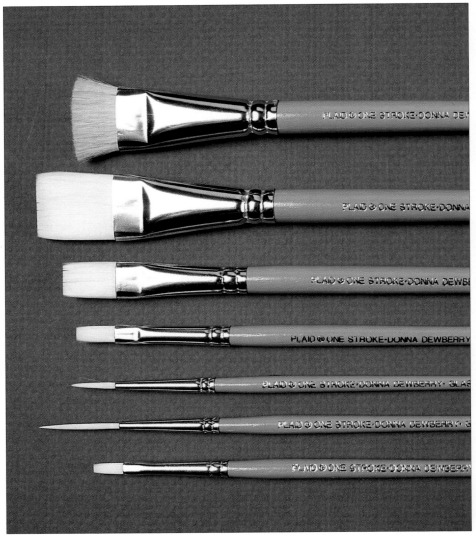

Parts of the Flat Brush

**The
Chisel Edge
(Bristle Tips)**

**Side
of
Brush Bristles**

**Flat
Part
of Brush**

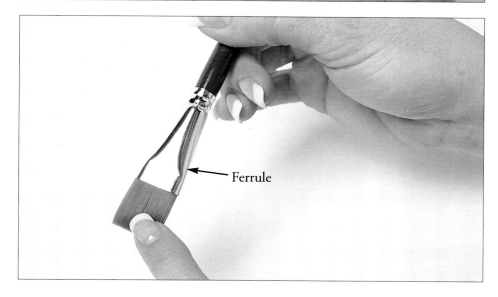

Ferrule

Cleaning Brushes

1. Dip brush in **Brush Plus® Brush Cleaner** (20480) and work the cleaner into the bristles.

2. Rinse the brush in water and rub the bristles back and forth across the bottom of the Brush Caddy basin, which has ridges to aid the cleaning process. Rinse until clean and dry the bristles on a paper towel.

3. Rub a little brush cleaner into the bristles to help the brush keep its shape. Reshape the bristles to their original form. Store. Before using again, dip brush in water and wipe on paper towel.

BACKGROUND EFFECTS

Here are some of the techniques and products I use to create backgrounds and special effects for my painted designs.

Basecoating

A smooth, beautiful basecoat of paint on your project surface is the perfect surface for decorative painting your flowers, birds, bees, and other One-Stroke designs. The large flat brushes are great for applying the basecoat to the surface. Be sure to prepare your surface appropriately, then add two to three coats of paint, allowing ample drying time between coats. Once your basecoated surface is dry and smooth, you can begin your decorative painting.

Choose a subtle color that is an enhancing backdrop for your painting, not one that calls attention to itself. You want your painted designs to be the star of the show.

A nice basecoated surface is also the foundation for creating the background effects explained shown in this chapter. This foundation basecoating is so important to the finished look of your project. As in building a house, always start with a good foundation.

Antiquing with Antiquing Polish

Use Antiquing Polish to add an aged look to painted surfaces. Antiquing Polish can safely be applied over paint (it won't lift the paint) or over varnish. It dries to a matte sheen and comes in Brown (590), Black (591), and White (592).

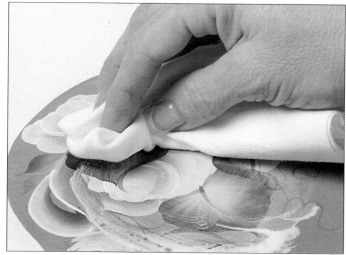

1. Squirt a puddle of Antiquing Polish on the painted, cured surface.

2. Using a soft cloth, rub the Antiquing Polish over the project to seal and polish. Use as much as you like to create a weathered look.

Crackled Backgrounds

You can use **FolkArt Crackle Medium** (694) to duplicate the look of weather and age on painted surfaces. See page 24 for an example.

1. Basecoat surface. Allow paint to dry and cure. Brush on Crackle Medium. (It dries clear.) The thicker the coat, the bigger the cracks; a thin coat produces thinner cracks. Allow Crackle Medium to dry.

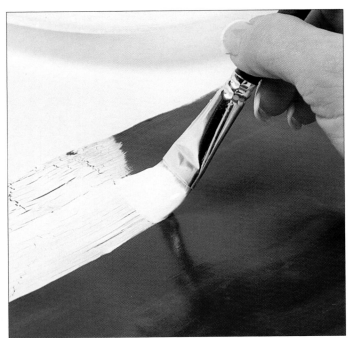

2. Brush on a substantial top coat of color. Cracks will form as the paint begins to dry.

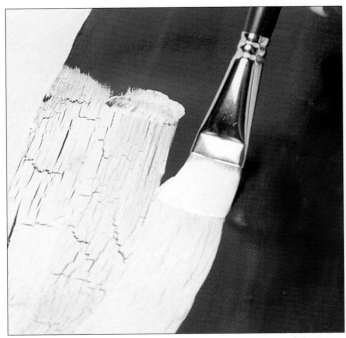

3. Continue to apply paint to the surface. Be careful not to overlap your strokes – overlapping can make the crackles disappear.

Sponged Backgrounds

Photo 1

My large Wall Faux Sponge or a kitchen sponge can be used to create a mottled/sponged background. Using a sponge is similar to using a scruffy brush – if you over-pounce or over-rub, you will muddy up the look. You want the colors to be distinct. (On a small project, you could use a scruffy brush instead of a sponge.)

1. Squeeze paint colors on your palette or a foam plate. Dampen the sponge in water and squeeze dry. Pounce half the sponge in one color and the other half in the second color. *(Photo 1)*
2. Put color on an area by pulling the sponge with a circular motion. *(Photo 2)*
3. Pat the sponge on the surface for a mottled look. Vary the placement of the sponge to avoid creating a repeated pattern. Re-load the sponge as it begins to lose its color. *(Photo 3)*

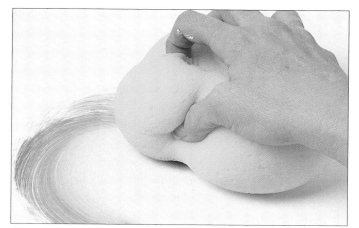

Photo 2

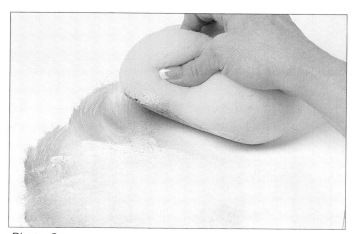

Photo 3

Basecoating a Large Area with a Sponge

You can use sponges for basecoating and for painting shapes:

For Basecoating: A Sponge Painter or a cellulose kitchen (household) sponge is a wonderful tool to use to apply a basecoat of color to a large design. Dampen the sponge with water and squeeze out the excess water. Load the entire sponge with color. You can pick up more than one color on the sponge. Rub the surface of the area in a circular motion to fill the area with paint.

For Painting Shapes: A sponge or Sponge Painters can be used to paint shapes such as a large flower pot, a vase on a wall, or the ground area of an landscape painting. Dampen the sponge and squeeze out the excess water. Load the entire dampened sponge with the color that is predominant. Then stroke the edge of the sponge into the shading color. Place the sponge on the surface, and use the edge of the sponge like a pencil to draw the shape of the element, adding pressure on

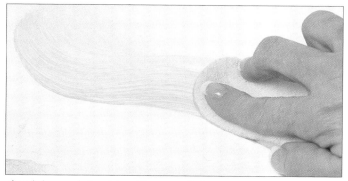

Applying paint with a Sponge Painter.

the edge with your fingers as you move the sponge along. I like to use this method also when I am painting creases in clothing or folds in a body.

Tip: Putting pressure on the straight edge of a sponge as you pull will create a straight line on an object.

Stenciling with a Sponge

Using a **Sponge Painter** (1195) for stenciling is quick and easy, and the sponge creates an interesting texture.

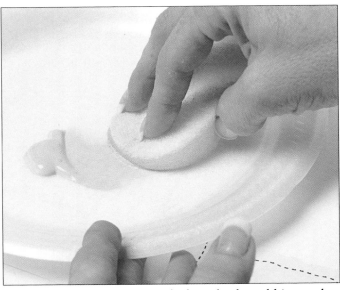

1. Load a Sponge Painter with the color by rubbing and pulling paint from a puddle on a foam plate.

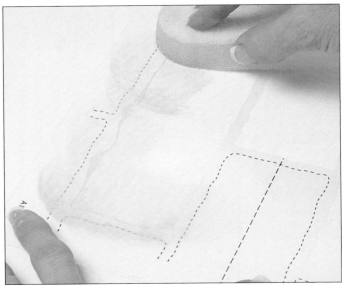

2. Lightly rub the sponge in a circular motion around the edges of the stencil openings.

Spattering

For spattering, I like to use an **old toothbrush**. This can get a bit messy, so be sure to protect your work surface with newspa-

1. Dip toothbrush into water.

2. Rub the wet brush in a circle at the edge of the paint puddle to make an inky mix of paint and fill the brush.

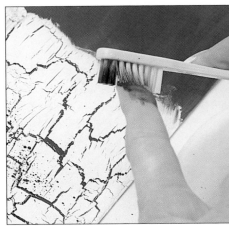

3. Hold the loaded brush over your project. Flick the brush with your finger, aiming the specks toward the project.

Background Effects Examples

PAINTING ON A CRACKLED BACKGROUND

This example shows how a painted design looks on a crackled and spattered background.

- **Basecoat** is Berry Wine.
- **Topcoat** is Wicker White.
- **Spattering** is with Burnt Umber.
- **Vines** - #12 flat with Burnt Umber and Linen.
- **Leaves** - #12 flat with Thicket, Burnt Umber, and Sunflower.
- **Curlicues** - #2 script liner with inky Burnt Umber.

PAINTING ON A SPONGED BACKGROUND

This example shows how a painted design looks on a sponged background. The colors used for sponging are Wicker White and Brilliant Ultramarine. Notice how the colors are not completely blended on the sponge.

- **Vines** - 3/4" flat with Burnt Umber and Linen.
- **Leaves** - 3/4" flat with Thicket, Burnt Umber, Sunflower, and Wicker White.
- **Shadow leaves and stems** - #12 flat with Floating Medium, Thicket, and Burnt Umber.
- **Curlicues** - #2 script liner with inky Burnt Umber.

LOADING YOUR BRUSH

This is most likely the most important aspect of learning to paint the One-Stroke technique. With a properly loaded brush, you can paint the various strokes with ease. Without a properly loaded brush, you won't be able to get through some of the strokes without your strokes fading out. Or starting your stroke smoothly without gobs of paint.

Double Loading a Flat Brush

#12 AND LARGER

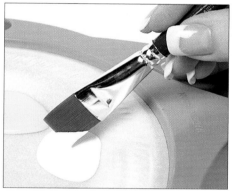

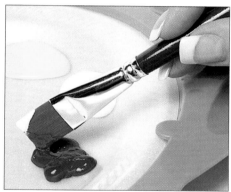

1. Dip brush in water. Blot it on paper towel.

2. Dip a corner of the brush in the first color. I usually like to dip in the light color first. Here, I am dipping in Wicker White.

3. Dip the opposite corner of the brush in the darker color. Here, the darker color is Berry Wine.

4. Stroke the brush between the two puddles. This spreads the paint in the brush and, at the same time, pulls more paint into the brush.

MANTRA

DIP

DIP

PAINT

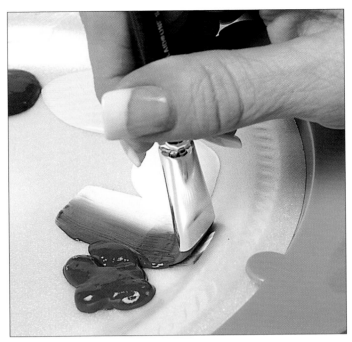

5. Stroke the brush back and forth on both sides to distribute paint into the bristles of the brush. Push hard to work in the paint.

6. Choose a different place on palette to continue to blend paint. Work paint into brush until brush is two-thirds full. Do not get paint into the ferrule. If needed, dip the corners of the brush in more paint to fully load the brush. Keep your blending area short – no longer than about 1-1/2".

7. After paint is worked in and brush is loaded, dip a tiny bit of the corner – the same corner as before – in the light color (Wicker White).

8. Dip a bit of the other corner in the darker color (Berry Wine).

9. Now you are ready to paint. Pull the brush across the surface on the flat side to make a flat stroke.

Double Loading a Flat Brush

#12 AND SMALLER

Smaller flat brushes are loaded differently. You first dip a corner of the brush in the dark color, then stroke into the light.

1. Pull the dark paint color from the edge of the puddle with the flat side of brush. Flip over the brush and pull paint with the other side.

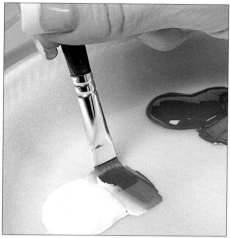

2. Position the brush on the edge of the light color and pull the side of the brush back and forth against the puddle.

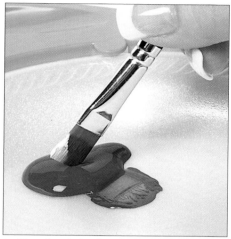

3. To reload the brush, dip the corner of the dark side of brush into the dark color.

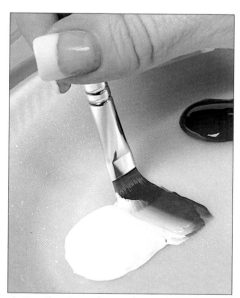

4. Stroke the other side in the light color.

5. Paint the stroke.

tips

- Remember to reload after each stroke.

- Remember to load smaller brushes differently than larger brushes.

for Loading a
Smaller Brush

MANTRA

DIP

STROKE

PAINT

Multi-Loading a Flat Brush

Multi-loading adds a third color to the brush.

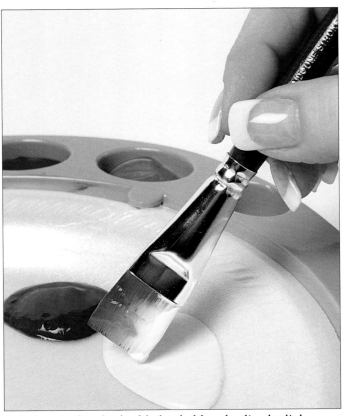

1. With an already double loaded brush, dip the light corner in the medium value color. Here, it is Sunflower.

2. Make stroke.

tips

• After each stroke you will need to reload your brush. To do this, simply dip the corners in the dark and light colors, then paint.

• Throughout this book, you will see little boxes with the word "Mantra" as a heading and some words below. These words are the ones I repeat to myself as I paint. For example, to remind myself to reload after each stroke, I say to myself, "Dip, Dip, Paint."

Multi-Loading
MANTRA

DIP

DIP

DIP

PAINT

Starter Stroke

Use these four steps to begin all the strokes you paint with your #12 flat brush or larger. The large brushes need lots of paint and the starter stroke spreads the bristles and blends the colors to achieve a smooth, blended stroke each time.

1. Double load your brush. Make guide marks with the chisel edge of the brush. Place the guide marks in a v-shape to begin and end the petal.

2. To start stroke, press down to spread the bristles and blend the paint.

3. Lift.

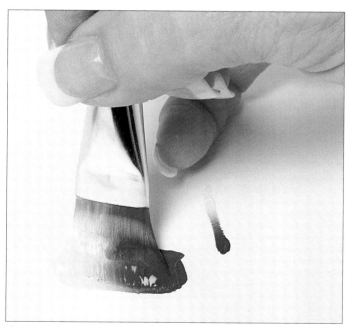

4. Press down again to spread the bristles and blend. Do this **THREE TIMES** in the same spot.

31

PAINTING WITH A FLAT BRUSH

The flat brush is the most versatile of the One Stroke brushes. As you will see in the following pages, the flat brush will allow you to paint everything – Roses, leaves, ribbons, bugs, and more. Their crisp chisel edges create clean, accurate strokes.

One Stroke flat brushes are ready to use from the package. Simply dampen the bristles in water and dry them with a paper towel before loading. When cleaning flat brushes, you can use the rake in the bottom of the Brush Caddy. Flat One Stroke brushes are synthetic and don't have a tendency to break, but be gentle.

A floral design painted with FolkArt® Acrylic Colors decorates this wooden box.

Correct Hand Position

It's important to hold the brush in your hand correctly.

Correct position. The wrist is free to move.

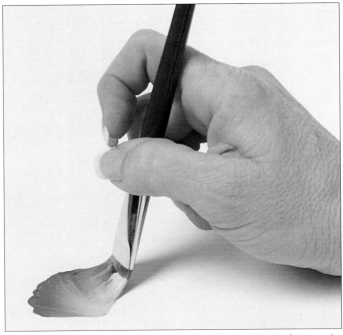

Incorrect position. The wrist is resting on the surface and can't move.

Pictured at right: This is the top of the wooden box shown on page 32, 33.

One Stroke Leaf

1. Load the brush with the leaf colors. Make an arrow with a pencil or with the chisel edge of your brush as guide marks.

2. Touch the loaded brush to the surface.

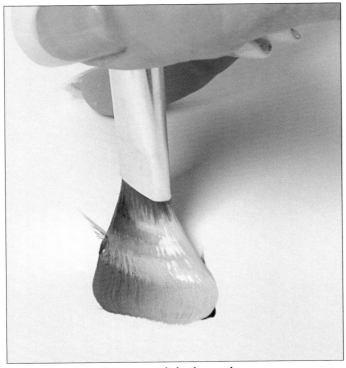

3. Push the bristles as you slide down the arrow.

4. Twist slightly to end the stroke with the brush on the chisel edge.

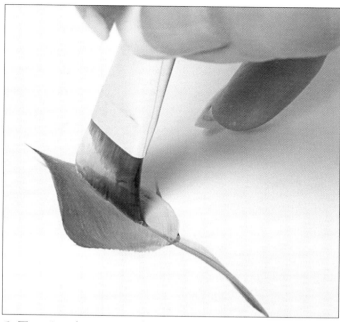

5. To paint the stem and vein, slide the brush into the leaf on the chisel edge.

Thanks

Thanks to Mary Ann Campbell for the tip on drawing an arrow to make guide marks for this leaf.

SUNFLOWER BUD WORKSHEET

The one stroke leaf can be used to paint a sunflower bud, as shown in this example.

Petals - #12 flat brush loaded with School Bus Yellow and Yellow Ochre.

Calyx and leaf - #12 flat loaded with School Bus Yellow and Thicket.

ONE STROKE LEAF WORKSHEET

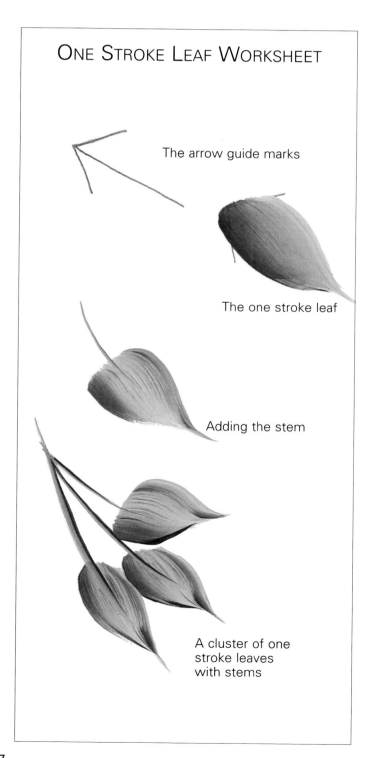

The arrow guide marks

The one stroke leaf

Adding the stem

A cluster of one stroke leaves with stems

Smooth Leaf Stroke

This stroke creates a **heart-shaped leaf**. The leaf is painted in two strokes.

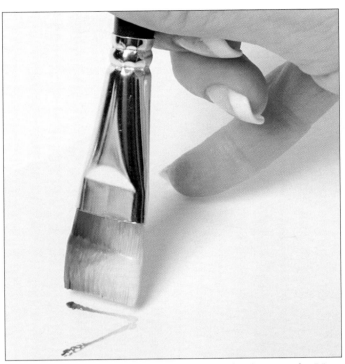

1. Double load your brush with the leaf colors. Make V-shaped guide marks for the top center of the leaf.

2. Start on the chisel edge of the brush at one of the guide marks.

3. Push down on the bristles as you curve the brush and pull.

4. To end, slide up to the chisel edge of the brush.

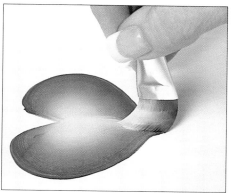

5. Complete the second half of the leaf in the same way, starting at the other guideline.

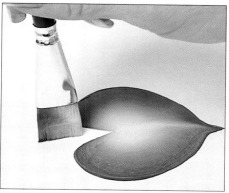

6. To create the stem and vein, touch the chisel edge of the brush to the surface.

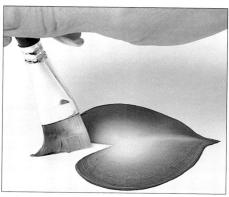

7. Tilt the brush back.

8. Pull the brush on the chisel edge to make the vein.

LEAF VARIATIONS WORKSHEET

Heart-shaped leaf - 3/4" flat brush loaded with Thicket and Sunflower.

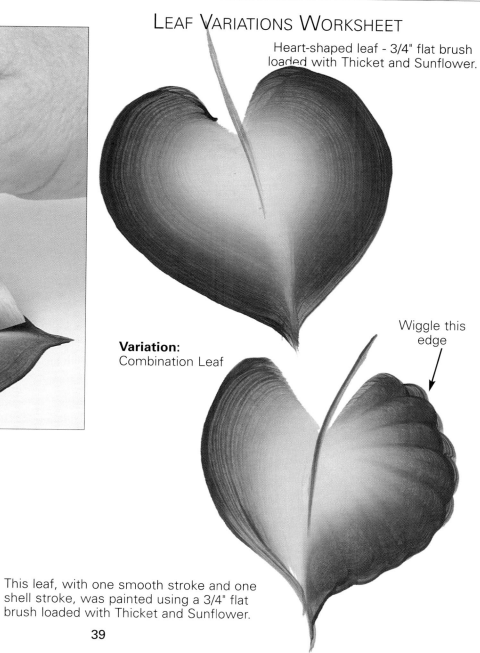

Variation: Combination Leaf

Wiggle this edge

This leaf, with one smooth stroke and one shell stroke, was painted using a 3/4" flat brush loaded with Thicket and Sunflower.

Shell Stroke

This stroke is used to paint **rose petals**. For examples, see the Rose Worksheet.

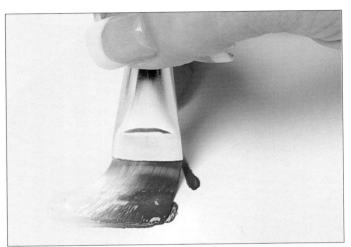

1. Wiggle the bristles in a scrubbing motion.

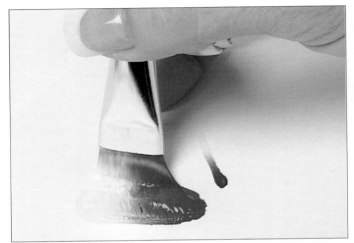

2. Continue wiggling the brush as you pull it along. You should be watching the white edge of the brush.

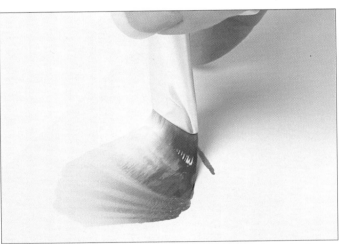

3. Wiggle the brush towards the guide mark, but don't angle the brush as you pull.

4. Pull the brush to the guide mark.

5. Slide down on the chisel edge to end the petal.

SHELL STROKE WORKSHEET

3/4" flat brush loaded with Berry Wine, Wicker White, and Sunflower.

40

ROSE WORKSHEET

3/4" flat brush and a 3/4" angle brush. Both were loaded with Berry Wine, Wicker White, and Sunflower.
See page 72 for information about using the angle brush.

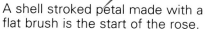

A shell stroked petal made with a flat brush is the start of the rose.

A second petal is painted next to the first one. Be sure to slightly overlap outer corners of the petals.

A circle of petals made with the flat brush forms the bottom layer.
A C-stroke and a U-stroke with an angle brush create the center.

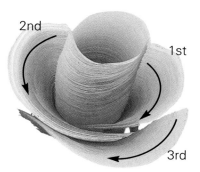

This example shows the strokes painted with the angle brush. Chisel slice strokes surround the center.

A second layer of slightly smaller petals is painted atop the first layer.

A wooden door plaque painted with flowers welcomes visitors. FolkArt® Lacquer protects the painted design from the weather.

Leaf Stroke

This stroke is used to make a **wiggle leaf**, commonly known as the rose leaf. One stroke is half the leaf.

1. Start by making a "Y" as guidelines. Double load your flat brush with the leaf colors. Make V-shaped guide marks with the chisel edge of the brush.

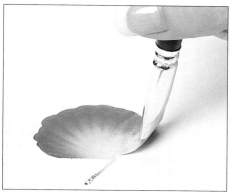

2. Start on one side of the V and pull the stroke, wiggling the brush as you go, until you see the sea shell shape. Pivot on the inside corner of the brush.

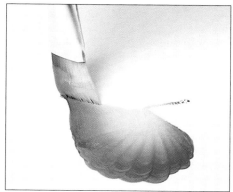

3. Slide the brush to make the tip of the leaf and pull to the chisel edge to end the stroke.

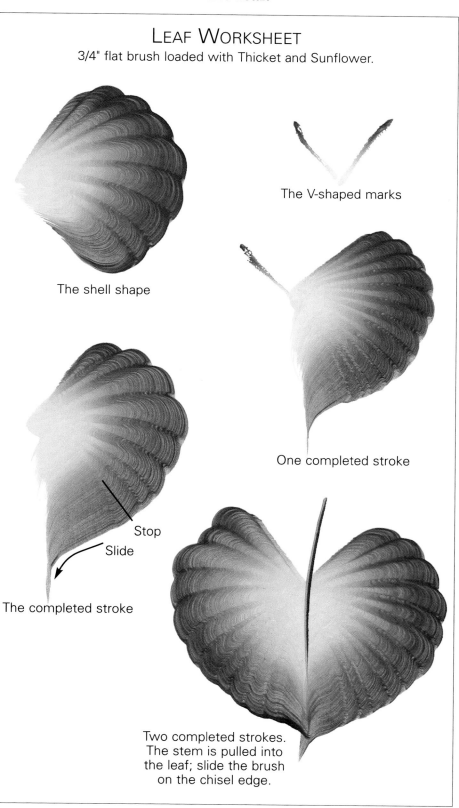

LEAF WORKSHEET
3/4" flat brush loaded with Thicket and Sunflower.

The shell shape

The V-shaped marks

One completed stroke

Stop

Slide

The completed stroke

Two completed strokes. The stem is pulled into the leaf; slide the brush on the chisel edge.

Turned Leaf

(A WIGGLE LEAF VARIATION)

1. Double load the brush with the leaf colors. Paint one side of the leaf. On the second side, paint the first third of the leaf and stop.

2. Roll the brush in your fingers so you're up on the chisel edge and the darker color is on the inner edge.

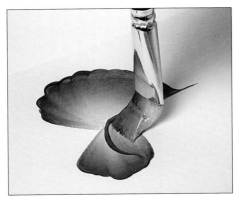

3. Apply pressure to the chisel edge as you pull the brush. This creates the turned effect.

TURNED LEAVES WORKSHEET

3/4" flat brush loaded with Thicket and Sunflower.

4. Continue the stroke, sliding the brush around.

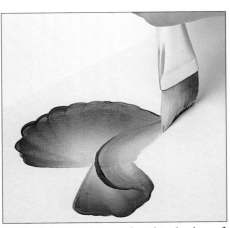

5. End the stroke on the chisel edge of the brush.

44

Ivy Leaf
(ANOTHER VARIATION OF THE WIGGLE LEAF)

The ivy leaf is painted with four strokes.

IVY LEAF WORKSHEET

To paint this leaf, load one side of a 3/4" flat brush with Thicket and Burnt Umber. Load the other side with Sunflower and Wicker White.

Completed ivy leaf - 3/4" flat brush loaded with Thicket and Sunflower.

This design features the Ivy Leaf as shown on page 45.

46

Looped Leaf

Used for the **sunflower leaf**.

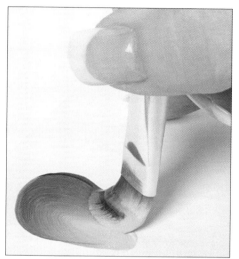

1. Load your brush with the leaf colors. Paint a teardrop stroke.

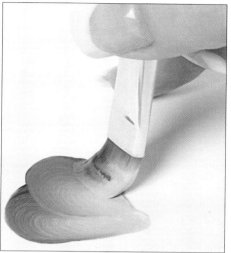

2. Paint overlapping teardrop strokes down one side of the leaf. Don't lift the brush at the end of each stroke.

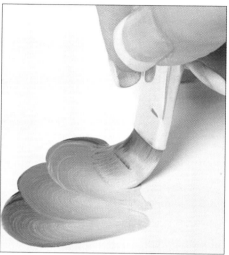

3. Continue to paint teardrop strokes without lifting the brush, making the strokes smaller as you get to the end of the leaf.

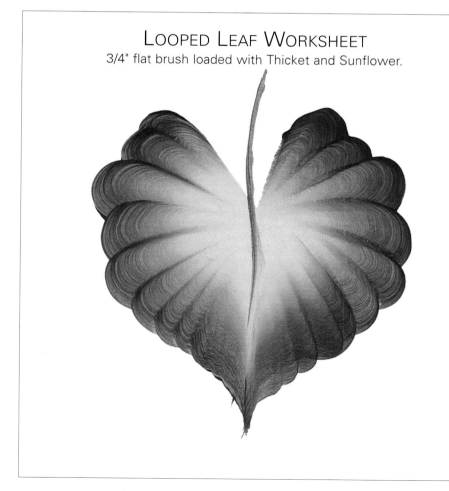

LOOPED LEAF WORKSHEET
3/4" flat brush loaded with Thicket and Sunflower.

4. End on the chisel edge of the brush as you pull to a point.

5. Paint the other side of leaf the same way.

Grape Leaf

This leaf is a variation of the **shell stroke**.

1. Load your flat brush with the leaf colors. Make V-shaped guide marks with the chisel edge of the brush. Start on one side of the V and pull the stroke, wiggling the brush as you go and ending on a point.

2. Reverse the direction of the bristles as you begin to slide to the center. Do not lift brush off your project.

3. Slide the brush to the center.

4. Reverse direction of the bristles again and begin to wiggle out to tip.

5. Slide the brush back to the center.

6. Reverse the direction of the bristles again and wiggle down the leaf.

7. End this side of the leaf by lifting to a point on the chisel edge of the brush.

GRAPE LEAF WORKSHEET
3/4" flat brush loaded with Thicket and Sunflower.

C-Stroke

This stroke is used to make **rosebuds**.

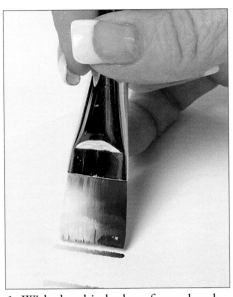

1. With the chisel edge of your brush, place two parallel lines to indicate the width of the rosebud. These lines will be your guide marks for beginning and ending the stroke on the chisel edge.

2. For the upper part of the bud, start the stroke with the brush on its chisel edge at one of the guide marks.

3. Push the bristles into a curve.

4. Pull up on the brush to end on the chisel edge at the other guide mark.

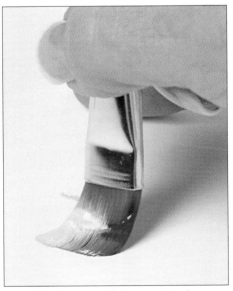

5. Make bottom of the rose in the same way. Touch on the chisel edge at one guide mark.

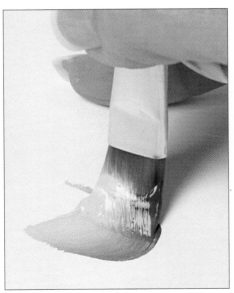

6. Push the bristles into a curve, then end on the chisel edge at the other guide mark.

Chisel Slice Stroke

This stroke is used to create a more open **rosebud**, one with some petals that have opened.

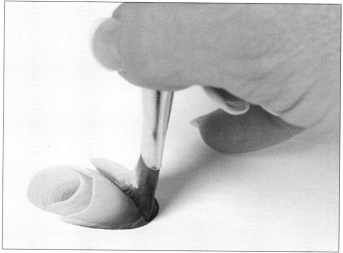

1. Pull the brush on chisel edge from one side across to the center of the rosebud.

2. This photo shows the stroke without the rosebud – touch, lean on chisel, and pull as you lift back to the chisel.

3. Paint the same kind of stroke on the other side, coming from that side to the center.

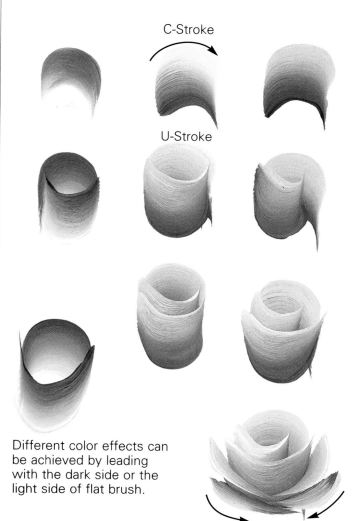

ROSEBUD WORKSHEET

#12 flat loaded with Berry Wine, Wicker White, and Sunflower.

C-Stroke

U-Stroke

Different color effects can be achieved by leading with the dark side or the light side of flat brush.

Chisel slice strokes

Teardrop Stroke

This stroke is used to paint **five-petal flowers**. Load the brush, following the instructions for the size brush you are using.

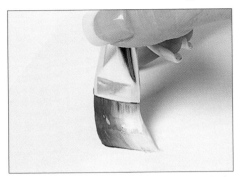

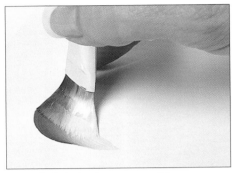

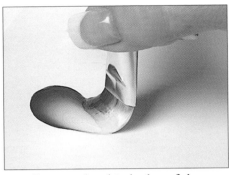

1. Touch the chisel edge of the loaded brush to the surface.

2. Push bristles in a curve. Do not turn the brush handle. Keep the dark side of brush on the outer edge of the flower petal to create the shape.

3. Pull up to the chisel edge of the brush and release pressure.

POINTED TEARDROP STROKE

This stroke is used for hydrangea blossoms

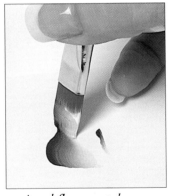

Use this stroke to paint a pointed flower petal.

1. Touch the chisel edge of the loaded brush to the surface.

2. Push bristles in a curve. Do not turn the brush handle. Keep the dark side of the brush on the outer edge.

3. Pull up to chisel edge and release pressure to make the point, then push bristles in a curve again for the second half of the petal. Pull up to the chisel edge and release the pressure to complete the stroke.

WORKSHEET
5–Petal Flower & Hydrangea Blossoms

Teardrop Stroke - #12 flat brush
Dioxazine Purple/Wicker White

Strokes create a 5-petal flower
Dot center -School Bus Yellow

Pointed Teardrop Stroke Four strokes create a hydrangea flower

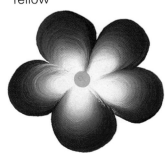

Comma Stroke

This stroke is used to make petals for flowers such as **daisies** and **chrysanthemums**.

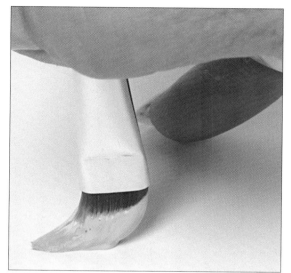

1. Touch the loaded brush to the surface and lean along chisel to spread bristles.

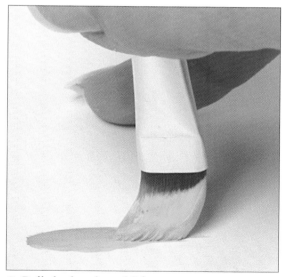

2. Pull the brush and lift.

COMMA STROKE WORKSHEET
3/4" flat loaded with School Bus Yellow, Yellow Ochre, and Wicker White.

Single stroke

One layer of petals forms daisy

1/2 view of daisy

Circle Stroke

This stroke is used for painting **grapes**.

1. Load brush with grape colors. Touch to surface and push down brush bristles.

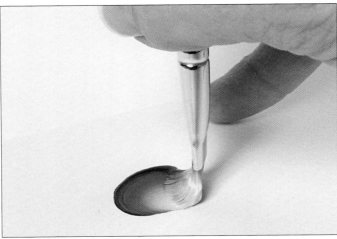

2. With the dark color on the outer edge, move the brush around to paint a half-circle.

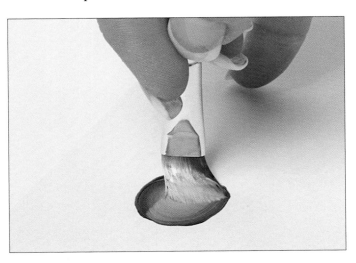

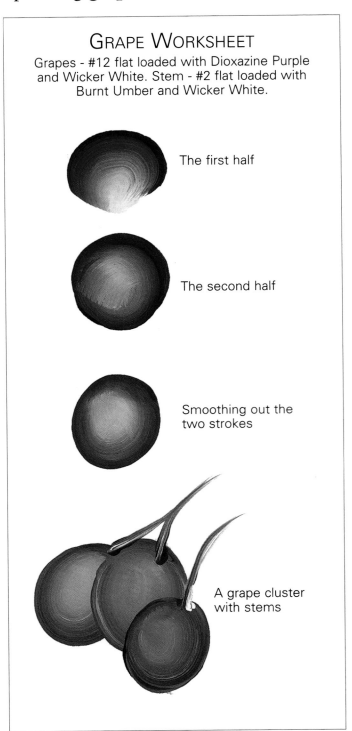

GRAPE WORKSHEET

Grapes - #12 flat loaded with Dioxazine Purple and Wicker White. Stem - #2 flat loaded with Burnt Umber and Wicker White.

The first half

The second half

Smoothing out the two strokes

A grape cluster with stems

3. Start the second half of the grape where you began first, pulling in other direction with the darker color on the outer edge. Go over the grape to smooth out and join the two strokes, using lighter pressure.

54

Chisel Edge Stroke

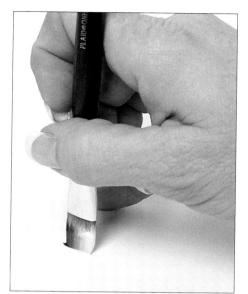

1. After brush is loaded, touch it to surface on chisel edge.

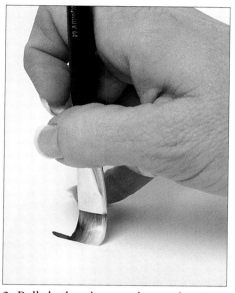

2. Pull the brush towards you, leaning the brush as you pull it to make the stroke.

Chisel Edge Stroke
MANTRA
TOUCH

LEAN

PULL

PLAID WORKSHEET

This plaid was painted using two sizes of flat brushes. The 3/4" flat brush was loaded with Berry Wine, Sunflower, and Floating Medium and pulled to create the large wide stripe of color. The #8 brush was loaded with Thicket and Floating Medium and pulled to make the medium stripe. The thinnest stripes were made by pulling the 3/4" brush on the chisel edge.

Chisel Edge Techniques

The chisel edge of a flat brush can be used for painting many things. You can use the brush single loaded or double loaded. I most often use it double loaded to add a nice color variation to the stroke when I paint **vines**, **leaf veins**, and **flower petals**.

PULLING

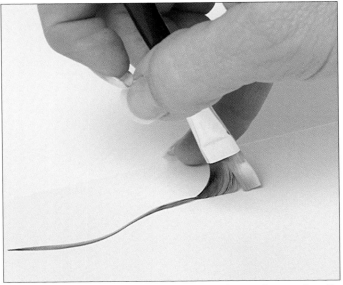

Touch the chisel edge of the brush to the surface and pull it along to paint vines.

DABBING

Touch the chisel edge of the brush to the surface and dab lightly to paint stalk flowers.

PUSHING AWAY

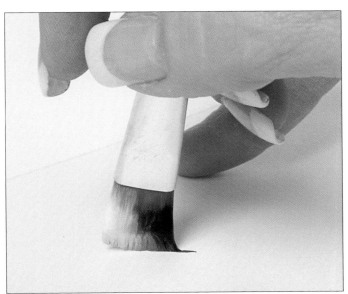

1. Touch chisel edge to surface and push away to paint a thistle, using a flicking kind of motion.

2. Add more strokes, using the same technique, to form the thistle.

56

VINES WORKSHEET

#12 flat brush loaded with Wicker White and Burnt Umber.

urliques are made with script liner and inky urnt Umber

STALK FLOWER WORKSHEET

Pulling stroke:
#12 flat brush with Wicker White, Sunflower, and Dioxazine Purple.

THISTLE WORKSHEET

#12 flat loaded with Dioxazine Purple and Wicker White. Use chisel edge, pushing away to make the stroke.

Color variations for stalk flowers #12 flat brush

Use a dabbing motion on the chisel edge

With Berry Wine/Wicker White/School Bus Yellow

With Berry Wine/ Wicker White/ Sunflower

With Berry Wine/ Wicker White/ Sunflower/ Dioxazine Purple

Ribbon Stroke

Using **Floating Medium** (868) in your brush will help the stroke flow better.

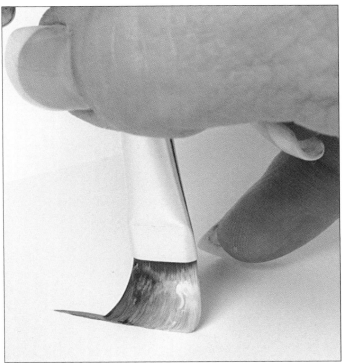

1. Load your flat brush with the ribbon colors. Start on the chisel edge.

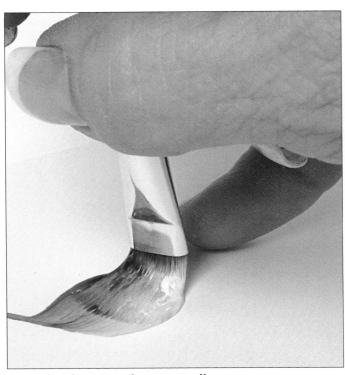

2. Lay brush on its side as you pull.

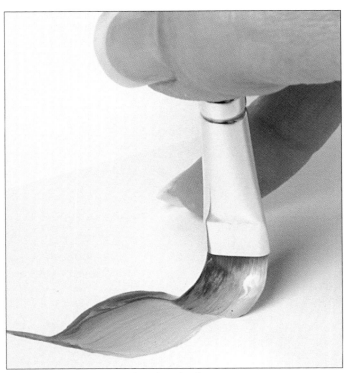

3. Bring brush up to the chisel edge.

4. Lay brush on its other side and pull.

RIBBON WORKSHEET

Use the ribbon stroke to paint a bow.
#12 flat brush is loaded with Berry Wine and Wicker White.

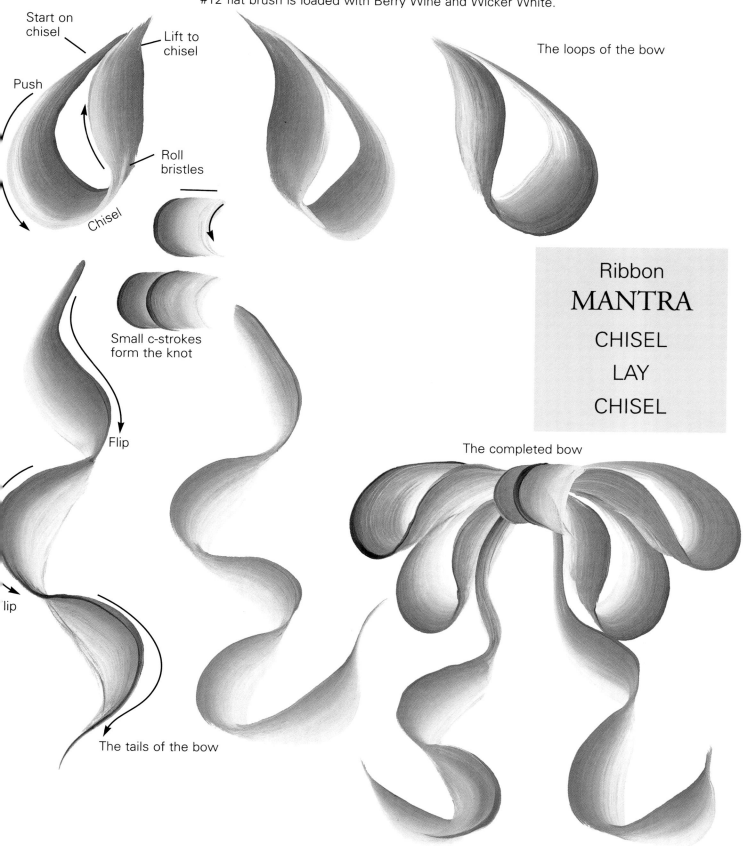

Start on chisel

Lift to chisel

Push

Roll bristles

Chisel

The loops of the bow

Small c-strokes form the knot

Ribbon
MANTRA
CHISEL
LAY
CHISEL

Flip

The completed bow

lip

The tails of the bow

LEAFY STALKS WORKSHEET

A variety of strokes can be used to paint leafy stalks.
#12 flat brush loaded with Thicket, Sunflower, and Wicker White. To start,
load the brush and paint the stalk on the chisel edge, then add the leaves.

Fig. 1 - Using a short pulling stroke.

Fig. 2 - Using a lightly curved teardrop stroke.

Fig. 3 - Using a one stroke leaf.

Fig. 4 - Using a pushing away stroke.

BUTTERFLY & DRAGONFLY WORKSHEET

BUTTERFLY

DRAGONFLY

Wings - #12 flat, Wicker White/Licorice

Wings
Use the "One-Stroke
Leaf" technique
#12 flat - Dioxazine
Purple/Wicker White

Touch

Pull

Lift on
chisel

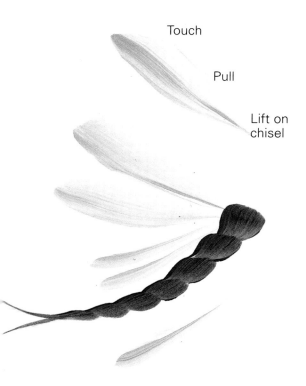

Body
#2 script liner - Thicket

Body
#12 flat - Night Sky/Thicket

PAINTING WITH THE SCRUFFY BRUSH

One Stroke scruffy brushes are ready to use.
All you have to do is "fluff the scruff" – remove the
brush from the packaging, form the bristles into
an oval shape by gently pulling them, and then twist
the bristles in the palm of your hand until they are
a nice oval shape. You're ready to pounce the
brush in paint and begin!
A fluffed scruffy brush is used to paint mosses, wisteria,
lilacs, and some hair and fur, faux finishes, and
shading textures.

Loading with Two Paint Colors

1. Squeeze small puddles of paint on your palette. Pounce one side of the brush at the edge of dark color paint puddle. Push hard to load paint.

2. Pounce other side of the brush into the light color. Pounce up and down on palette to load paint and distribute the paint through the bristles.

3. A properly loaded brush.

Painting

1. Pounce brush on surface, but be careful not to over-pounce so the colors will remain separate, not muddy-looking and blended.

2. To add additional colors for a multi-loaded brush, pounce the brush into a third color. If it is a dark color, load it on the dark side of brush.

3. Load another light color on the light side.

4. Pounce on the surface to paint.

SCRUFFY BRUSH TECHNIQUE WORKSHEET

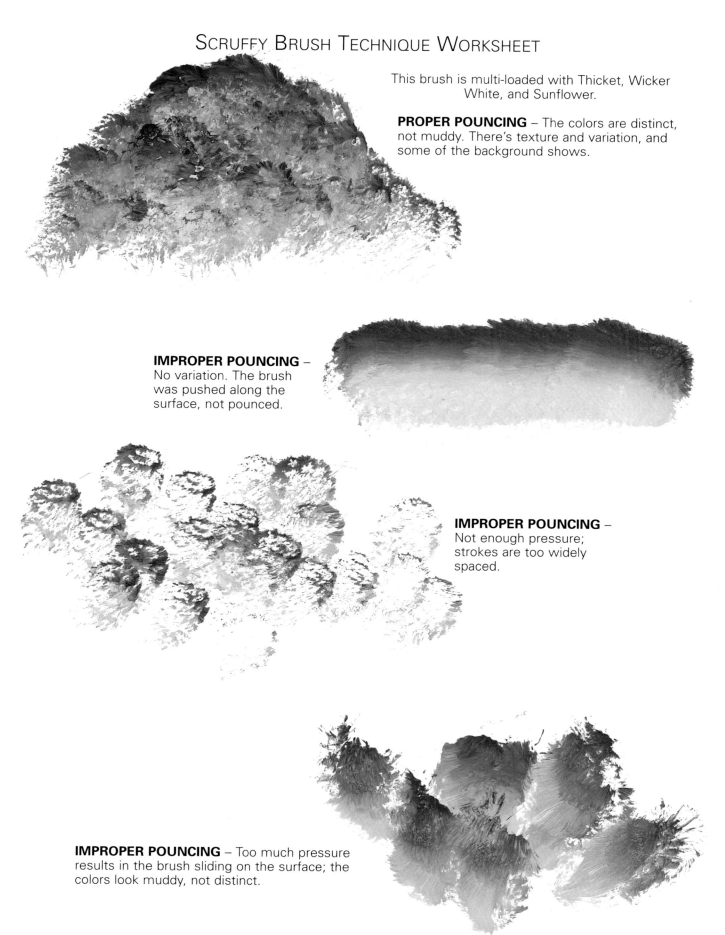

This brush is multi-loaded with Thicket, Wicker White, and Sunflower.

PROPER POUNCING – The colors are distinct, not muddy. There's texture and variation, and some of the background shows.

IMPROPER POUNCING – No variation. The brush was pushed along the surface, not pounced.

IMPROPER POUNCING – Not enough pressure; strokes are too widely spaced.

IMPROPER POUNCING – Too much pressure results in the brush sliding on the surface; the colors look muddy, not distinct.

Painting with a Liner Brush

Liner brushes are used to paint details, accents, curlicues, and ribbons. They are used with paint that is inky (thinned with water to the consistency of ink). You can also use a liner brush to sign your work, like I do!

These ceramic tiles were painted with FolkArt® Enamels.

Loading a Liner Brush

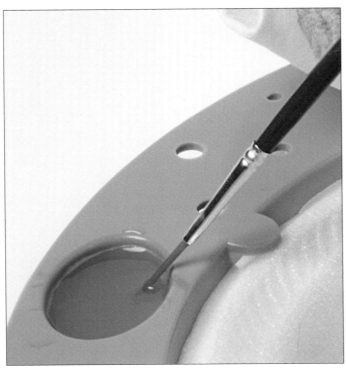

1. Dip brush in water.

2. Lay bristles next to a puddle of paint and touch tip of brush in paint.

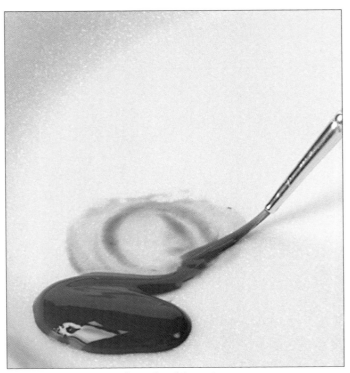

3. Move tip in a circle to load in paint.

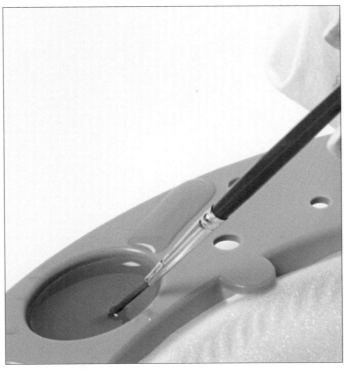

4. Dip brush back in water.

5. Continue making a circle to create an inky puddle of paint and load the brush. Do this a total of three times.

6. Roll the brush out of the paint puddle as you twist the bristles to a point.

Painting with a Liner Brush

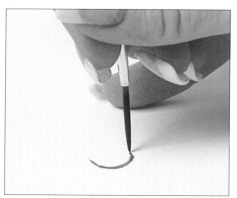

1. Paint with only the tips of the bristles touching the surface.

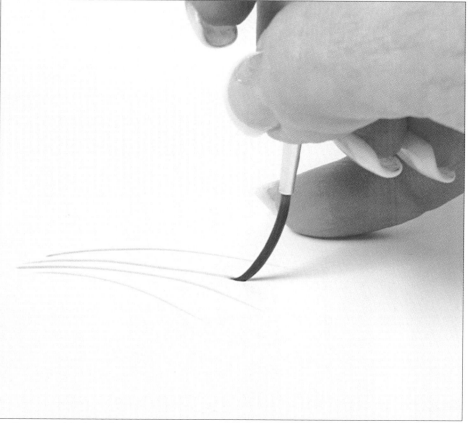

2. Painting curlicues. Move brush along on its tip.

3. Painting blades of grass. Notice the hand position – your finger guides the brush. The brush is held in a vertical position – no leaning.

Pressure Stroke #1

Used for Butterfly Bodies, Grasses, Flower Petals

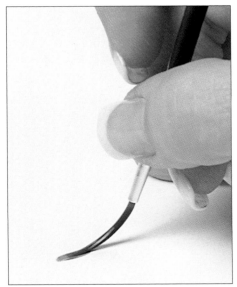  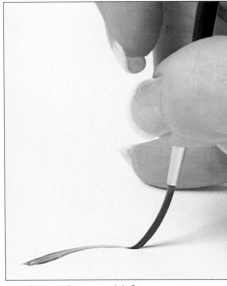

1. Push brush on surface.

2. Lift brush as you pull.

3. The pushing and lifting creates a comma stroke.

Pressure Stroke #2

Used for Butterfly Antennae

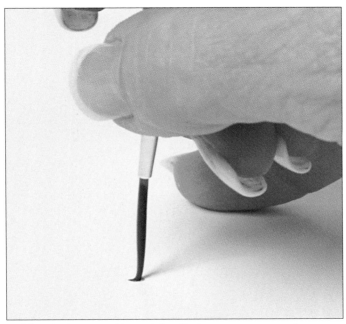 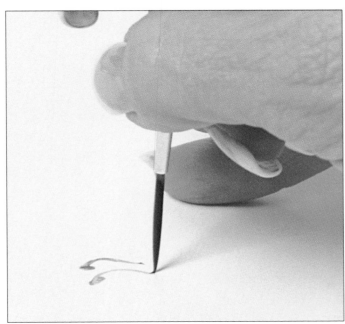

1. Touch tip to surface with a little pressure to make a dot.

2. Release pressure as you pull and lift on the tip.

LINER BRUSH WORKSHEET

Curliques
#2 script liner with Thicket

Scrolls
#2 script liner with Thicket

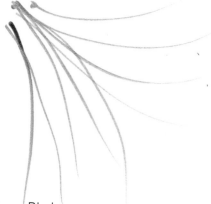

Grass Blades
#2 script liner with Thicket

Butterfly
#2 script liner with Thicket (body & antennae)
#12 flat with Dioxazine Purple/Wicker White (wings)

Comma Strokes and Lettering
#2 Script liner with Thicket

Cross Hatching
#2 script liner with Yellow Ochre

String Bow
#2 script liner with Dioxazine Purple

Comma Strokes
#2 script liner with Yellow Ochre

71

PAINTING WITH AN ANGLE BRUSH

An angle brush is similar to a flat brush, but the bristles of the angle brush are trimmed at an angle. On the following pages, you'll see how I use angle brushes in the One Stroke technique.
This brush is a secret weapon for making perfect comma strokes on the cabbage rose.

A rose in full bloom is the centerpiece of this design painted on a tin pitcher with FolkArt® Enamels™.

Loading the Brush

Determine the color you wish to lead with. That color will be
the second color you load into the brush. For this example,
I chose to lead with the darker color.

1. Dip the toe of the brush in the lighter color.

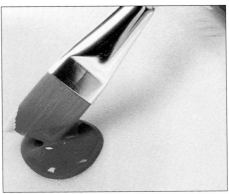

2. Dip the other corner (heel) into the darker color (the color I want to lead with).

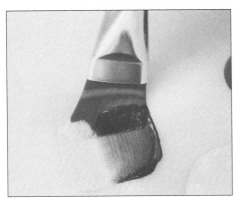

3. Work the brush back and forth on the palette.

4. Pick up more of the lighter color.

5. Pick up more of the darker color.

6. Work the brush back and forth again on the palette. Keep the space where you are loading and working brush small. Load the brush until it is two-thirds full.

Angle Brush Strokes

Toe →
Heel →

This example shows the angle brush being used to
create the petals around the **center of the rose**.
The shell-shaped outer petals (around the outside of
the rose) are made with the flat brush.

1. Touch the brush to the surface.

2. Lean the brush out.

3. Pull the brush to the chisel edge, ending on the light tip.

4. Paint the same stroke on the other side of the bud.

ROSE WORKSHEET

Middle petals - 3/4" angle brush.
Berry Wine, Wicker White, and Sunflower.

5. Lean and pull.

6. End on the chisel edge.

Painting a Rosebud

The angle brush can be used to paint an entire **rosebud** or small **open rose**.

1. Load your brush and start the rose with wiggle stroke petals.

2. Add a tight C-stroke to form the top petal of the bud.

3. Add a tight U-stroke under the C-stroke to form the lower petal of the bud.

4. Start a side petal by leaning out with the brush.

5. Turn and roll the brush.

6. Continue the stroke, coming across the bottom of the bud.

7. Make strokes under the bud, working on the chisel edge of the brush.

SMALL ROSE WORKSHEET

An angle brush loaded with Berry Wine, Wicker White, and Sunflower was used to paint these small roses.

(1) A small rose. The outer petals are painted on the chisel edge of the brush.

(2) A rose in progress

(3) The wiggle stroke petals that start the rose

(4) The C-stroke and tight U-stroke are added to form the center bud

(5) More strokes are added.

Painting a Rose Calyx

Adding Floating Medium to your brush helps in painting the long, curvy strokes.

1. Load the brush with the leaf colors and Floating Medium. With brush on the chisel edge, touch the surface and lean forward.

2. Pull and end the stroke at the top.

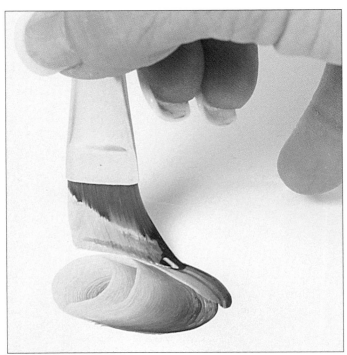

3. Pulling the calyx stroke on one side of the rose.

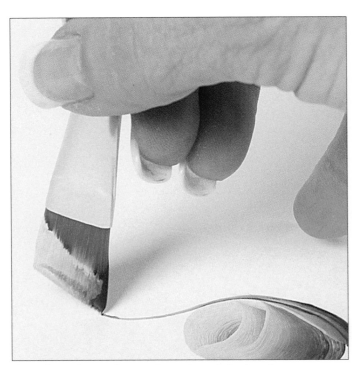

4. Ending the stroke on the point of the brush.

5. Stroking the other side.

6. Add a smaller stroke (or strokes) at the center of the calyx.

CALYX WORKSHEET

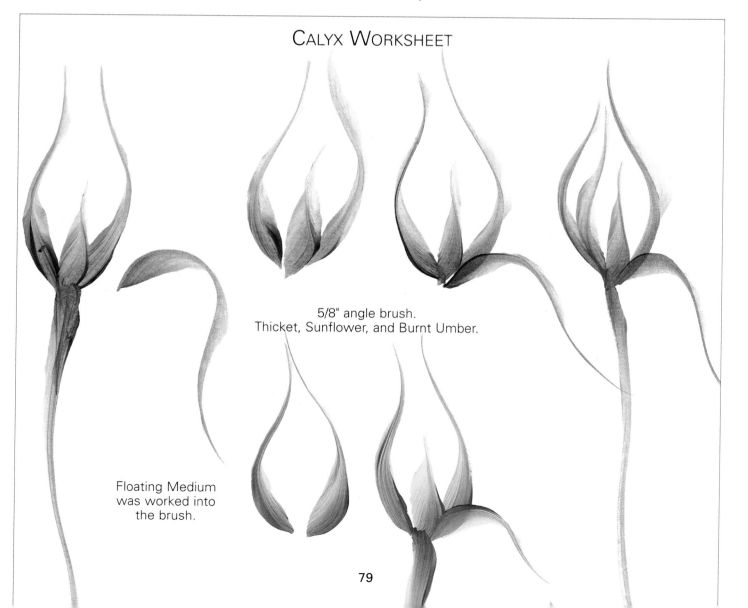

5/8" angle brush.
Thicket, Sunflower, and Burnt Umber.

Floating Medium was worked into the brush.

Ribbon Stroke

Curving ribbons can be painted with an angle brush. Use Floating Medium in your brush to help the paint flow smoothly.

1. Touch the loaded brush to the surface.

2. Lean and slide the brush.

3. Pull up to the chisel edge.

4. Lean the brush the other way and continue to slide.

RIBBON WORKSHEET
5/8" angle brush with Berry Wine, Wicker White, and Floating Medium.

VINES WORKSHEET
5/8" angle brush with Thicket, Sunflower, and Burnt Umber.

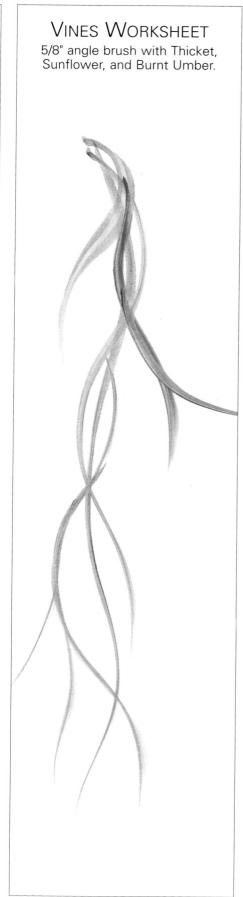

Painting Vines

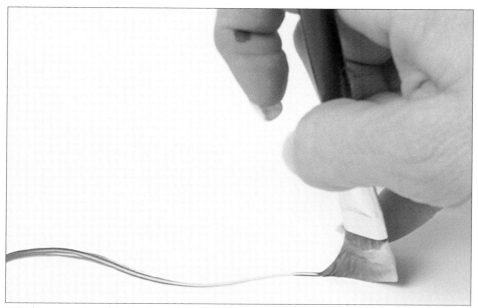

Working on the chisel edge of the brush, pull. Lead with the light color.

Painting a Bent Leaf

I use this technique for painting tulip and iris leaves.

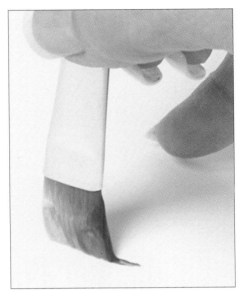

1. Load the brush with leaf colors. Begin on the chisel edge.

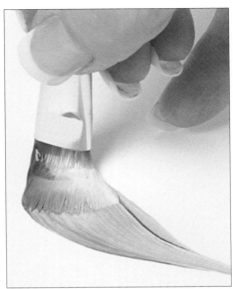

2. Push up onto the flat side of the brush.

3. Bring the brush back up to the chisel edge.

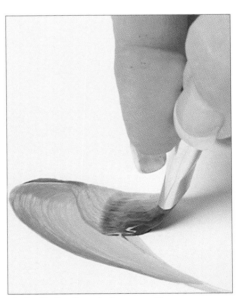

4. Roll the brush in your fingers.

5. Pull the brush straight down and lift to complete the stroke.

BENT LEAF WORKSHEET

Various examples of bent leaves.
5/8" angle brush - Thicket, Wicker White, and Sunflower.

ANGLE BRUSH WORKSHEET
Here are some examples of what you can paint with an angle brush.

(1) Grass
5/8" angle brush loaded with Thicket
and Sunflower

(2) Wiggle leaves
5/8" angle brush loaded with Thicket
and Sunflower

(3) Wiggle leaves
5/8" angle brush loaded with Thicket and Sunflower

(4) One stroke leaves
3/8" angle brush loaded with Thicket and Sunflower

(5) Small wiggle leaves
3/8" angle brush loaded with Thicket and Sunflower

(6) Stem and thorns
3/8" angle brush loaded with Thicket and Sunflower

PAINTING WITH A FILBERT BRUSH

A filbert brush is similar to a flat brush, but the bristles of the filbert brush are slightly tapered. On the following pages, you'll see how I use filbert brushes in the One Stroke technique. This brush smooths the edges of your One Stroke leaves. It also makes wonderful daisies, chrysanthemums and hydrangeas.

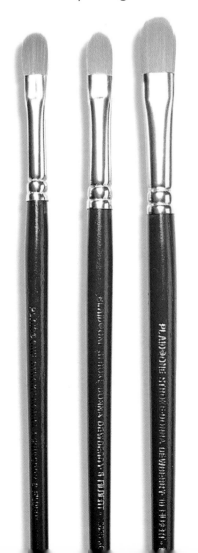

A filbert brush is used to paint chrysanthemums.

Loading

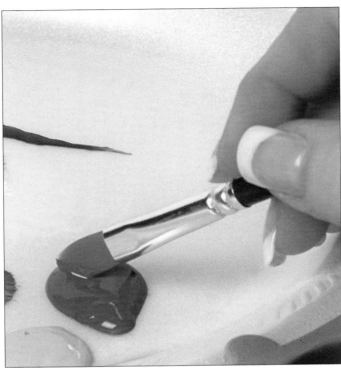

1. Dip one side of the brush in the dark paint color.

2. Turn brush and dip other side in the light paint color.

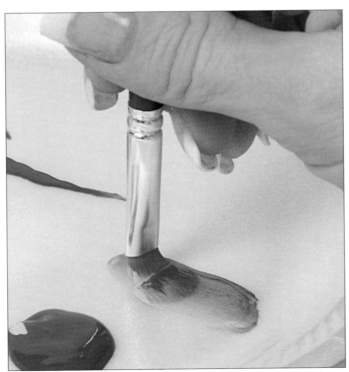

3. Stroke brush on palette to work paint into the brush.

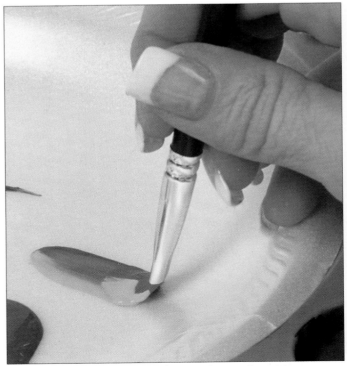

4. Turn brush over and work paint into other side. Continue dipping in paint and stroking on the palette for a total of three times.

Teardrop Stroke

VERSION 1

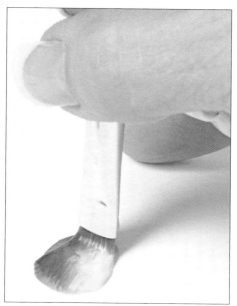 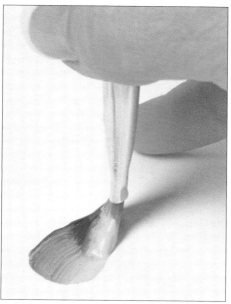 

1. Push brush down on its flat side.

2. Turn the brush slightly as you begin to decrease pressure and lift.

3. Pull to the edge of the brush and lift.

FIVE PETAL FLOWERS WORKSHEET

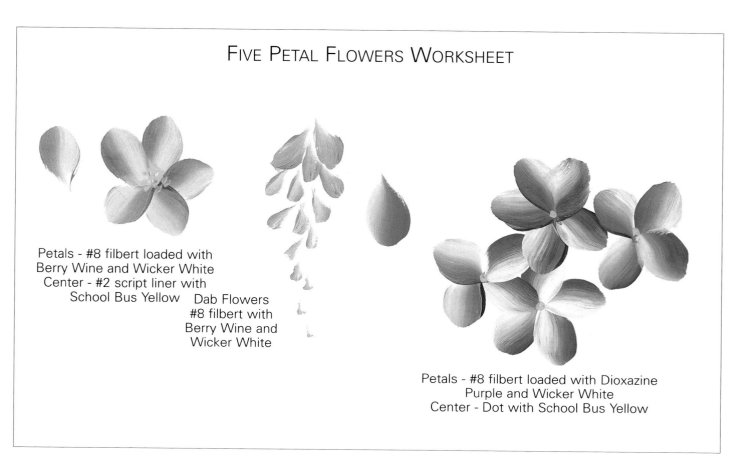

Petals - #8 filbert loaded with Berry Wine and Wicker White
Center - #2 script liner with School Bus Yellow

Dab Flowers #8 filbert with Berry Wine and Wicker White

Petals - #8 filbert loaded with Dioxazine Purple and Wicker White
Center - Dot with School Bus Yellow

Teardrop Stroke

VERSION 2

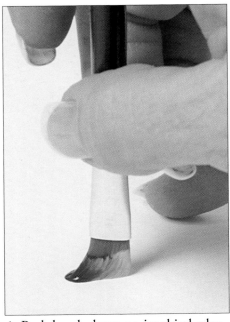

1. Push brush down on its chisel edge.

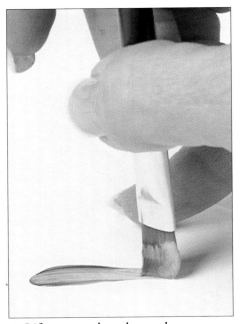

2. Lift to complete the stroke.

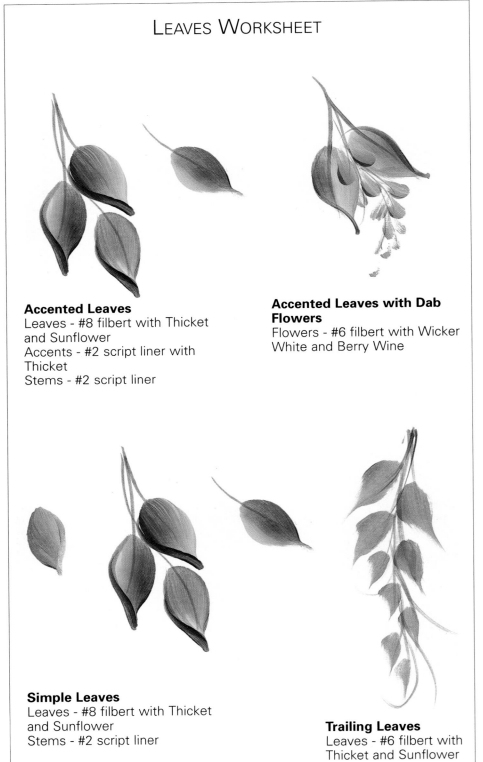

LEAVES WORKSHEET

Accented Leaves
Leaves - #8 filbert with Thicket and Sunflower
Accents - #2 script liner with Thicket
Stems - #2 script liner

Accented Leaves with Dab Flowers
Flowers - #6 filbert with Wicker White and Berry Wine

Simple Leaves
Leaves - #8 filbert with Thicket and Sunflower
Stems - #2 script liner

Trailing Leaves
Leaves - #6 filbert with Thicket and Sunflower plus Floating Medium
Stems - #2 script liner

DAISY & CHRYSANTHEMUM WORKSHEET

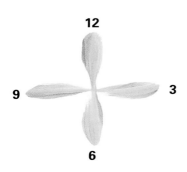

The first four daisy petals are spaced like a clock face.

Daisies
Petals - #8 filbert with Yellow Ochre and School Bus Yellow
Centers - Dot(s) of Burnt Umber

Daisy
Petals - #6 filbert with Sunflower and Wicker White
Center - Dots of Thicket

Chrysanthemums
Petals - #8 filbert with School Bus Yellow, Yellow Ochre, Wicker White
Stem and calyx - #2 script liner with Thicket and Sunflower

Daisy with Leaves and Stem
Petals - #8 filbert with Yellow Ochre and School Bus Yellow
Center - Dot of Wicker White
Leaf - #8 filbert with Thicket and Wicker White/Sunflower
Stem- #2 script liner with Thicket and Sunflower

91

PAINTING WITH A FAN BRUSH

A fan brush, which takes its name from its fan shape,
can be used to paint tree foliage, grasses,
flowers, and waves in the water. Pulling strokes
and dabbing strokes create the various
fan brush effects.

Loading

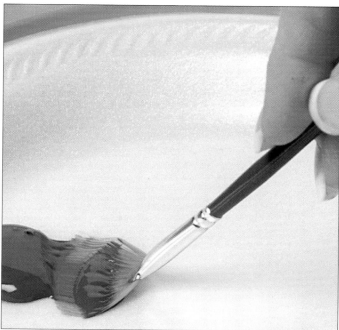

1. Pull paint from the edge of the paint puddle into the bristles. Load only about one-third of the length of the bristles.

2. Pull the second color into the brush on one side of brush.

Painting With Un-thinned Paint

Apply paint with a dabbing motion.

Use a pulling motion to paint items such as the foliage of evergreen trees.

Use the dabbing motion and white paint to add snow to the evergreen tree.

The dabbing motion also can produce flowers.

TWO TREES WORKSHEET

The foliage of these two trees and the snow of the evergreen tree are painted with a fan brush.

Leafy Tree
Foliage - Thicket, Sunflower, and Wicker White
Trunk - Burnt Umber and Wicker White
#12 flat brush

Evergreen Tree
Foliage - Thicket, Sunflower, and Wicker White
Snow - Wicker White

95

Painting With Thinned Paint

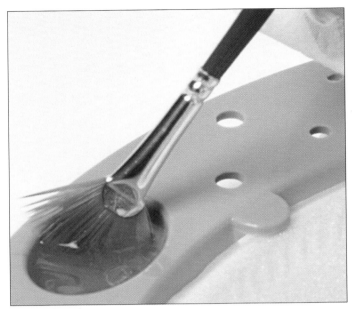

1. Dip brush in water.

2. Pull paint from a puddle into the brush bristles.

Paint grass by pulling on the flat side of brush.

Or by pulling on the edge of the brush.

Adding texture to a leaf with a fan brush.

GRASS & WILDFLOWERS WORKSHEET
Here, the fan brush is used to paint blades of grass and dabbed stalk flowers.

Grass - Thicket and Sunflower

Flowers - School Bus Yellow and Wicker White, Dioxazine Purple and Wicker White, Berry Wine and Wicker White

WAVES WORKSHEET
The fan brush can be used to paint waves and water.

Waves - Ultramarine Blue and
Wicker White
Foam - Wicker White

USING FLOATING MEDIUM

I use Floating Medium in my brush to make the paint flow easier.
I do this most often if I am painting long strokes like the ones for
ribbons or long leaves. You may also need to use Floating Medium
if you are painting on a rough or more porous surface where the paint
doesn't want to move. Having Floating Medium in your brush
helps move the brush smoothly and evenly.
These Floating Medium techniques are most often used with flat,
filbert, and angle brushes.

Loading a Brush with Floating Medium

Please **don't** follow the instructions on the bottle when using Floating Medium with the One Stroke Technique – if you do, your strokes will be muddy. Reload the brush with Floating Medium every third or fourth stroke; load paint with every stroke.

1. Squeeze a puddle of Floating Medium on your palette. Load brush and blend properly. Dip the tips of the bristles of the loaded brush straight down in the puddle of Floating Medium.

2. Take brush to another place on the palette and stroke to work the Floating Medium into the brush.

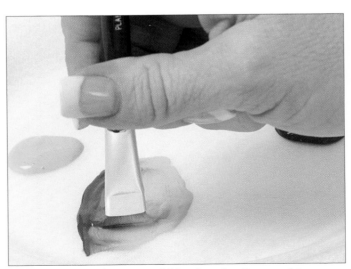

3. Turn the brush over and blend again. Repeat this procedure three times until you have an adequate amount of medium in brush. You're ready to paint.

Floating Shading

1. Load a clean brush with Floating Medium.

2. Stroke the side of the brush into paint.

DOGWOOD WORKSHEET

Dogwood petals are painted using a #12 flat brush loaded with Berry Wine and Wicker White. The center is pounced with School Bus Yellow and Berry Wine.

Paint petal.

3. Shade the desired area.

FLOATING A SHADOW

Float shading on rounded edges of petals with Berry Wine.

Shadows can be floated around the outside of the leaf, using the shading technique with Floating Medium. The side of the brush that is loaded with color is against the edge of the leaf.

Making Shadow Leaves

Shadow leaves are the background leaves I paint after the main part of my painting is complete – I use shadow leaves to fill in space and give the painting depth. These leaves are lighter and "dirtier," so that they appear to be in the background.

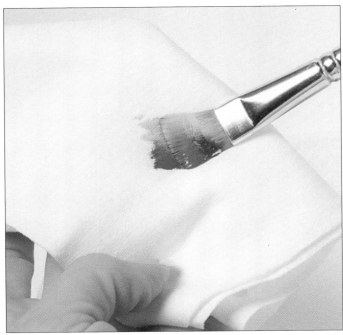

1. After you finish painting the regular leaves, wipe your brush on a paper towel to remove excess paint. **Do not** wash the brush – you want a "dirty" brush for painting shadow leaves.

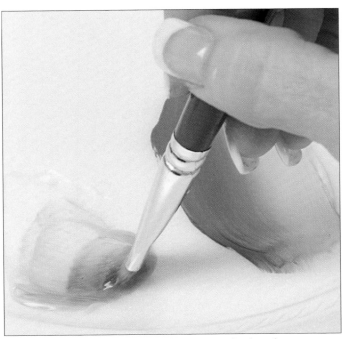

2. Pull and dab Floating Medium into the brush to get a transparent, dirty color.

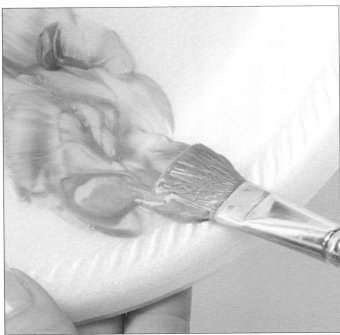

3. Scrape off the excess paint + Floating Medium as you pull the brush out of the paint.

4. Paint the shadow leaves.

SHADOW LEAF WORKSHEET

One-Stroke Leaf Technique

Center Leaves - #12 flat - Thicket, Burnt Umber, and Sunflower.
Shadow leaves - #12 flat - dirty brush loaded with Floating Medium to
create a transparent dirty color.

WISTERIA WORKSHEET

Vines
#12 flat loaded with Hunter Green, Wicker White, and School Bus Yellow.

On chisel edge

Cross over

Leaves
#12 flat with Hunter Green, Wicker White, and School Bus Yellow

Push, wiggle, slide

Start

End

Push, turn, lift

Start

End

Stem on chisel edge

Small Leaves
#8 flat with Hunter Green

Push, slide

On chisel

Wisteria
Scruffy with Dioxazine Purple, Cobalt, and Wicker White

1
2
3
4
5
6

Pounce

Curlicues
#2 script liner with inky Hunter Green

Start
Push, slide

102

Purple Pansy - Upper Petals
#12 flat with Dioxazine Purple and Wicker White

Start · End · 1

Start · End · 2

Start · 3

Bud

Touch, lean, and pull · 3

1

2

Purple Pansy - Lower Petals
#12 flat with Dioxazine Purple and School Bus Yellow

Push, slide

Reverse to Wicker White on outside of middle petals

4 · 5 · 7 · 6

Center
#6 flat with Hunter Green and School Bus Yellow

Dot - School Bus Yellow

On chisel

Stem

touch, lean, pull

Pink Pansy
#12 flat with Fuchsia and Wicker White

Blue Pansy
#12 flat with Cobalt and Wicker White

Large Leaves
#2 flat with Hunter Green and Grass Green

Push, wiggle, slide

Start

Start

End

Stem on chisel edge

Small Leaves

Push, turn, lift to chisel

Start

103

STRAWBERRY WORKSHEET

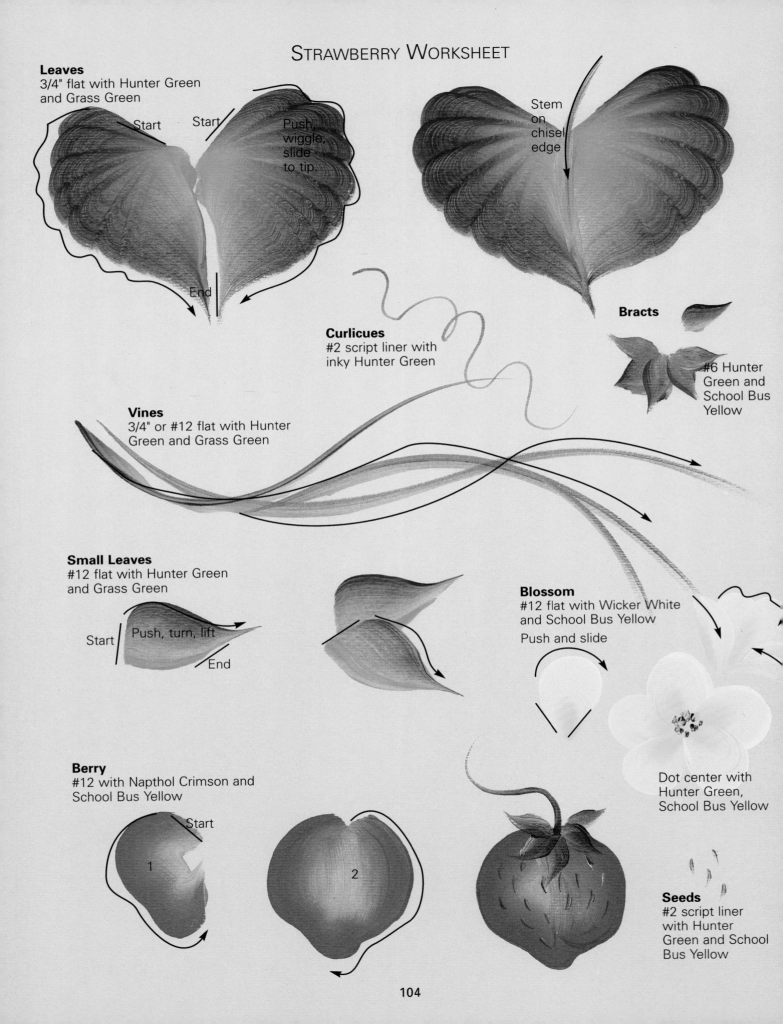

Leaves
3/4" flat with Hunter Green and Grass Green

Start

Start

Push, wiggle, slide to tip.

End

Stem on chisel edge

Bracts
#6 Hunter Green and School Bus Yellow

Curlicues
#2 script liner with inky Hunter Green

Vines
3/4" or #12 flat with Hunter Green and Grass Green

Small Leaves
#12 flat with Hunter Green and Grass Green

Start

Push, turn, lift

End

Blossom
#12 flat with Wicker White and School Bus Yellow

Push and slide

Dot center with Hunter Green, School Bus Yellow

Berry
#12 with Napthol Crimson and School Bus Yellow

Start

1

2

Seeds
#2 script liner with Hunter Green and School Bus Yellow

104

Apple
3/4" flat with Napthol Crimson and School Bus Yellow

Start

Push, turn

1

Start

2   3

Fill in

4

3/4" flat with
Napthol Crimson -
pull on chisel edge

Pear

Start

3/4" flat with
School Bus
Yellow and
Napthol
Crimson + a
touch of Burnt
Umber

1

End

Start

3

fill in   2

4

Touch stem end
with Hunter Green,
using #2 script liner

um
4" flat with Cobalt, Dioxazine
rple, Wicker White

Start

1

End

Start

2

Start

3

105

LARGE FLAT BRUSH WORKSHEET

Everything on this worksheet was painted using the 1" flat brush loaded with Green Forest and Yellow Light

2 Push and pull

1
Stem

Re-stroke stem to finish

3

Push & pull

Overlap strokes

Scruffy Brush Worksheet

Pouncing with a double-loaded scruffy (Thicket, Wicker White)

Pouncing with a multi-loaded scruffy (Thicket, Burnt Umber, Wicker White, Sunflower)

The scruffy brush is used to pounce the centers of sunflowers. Load scruffy with Burnt Umber and Licorice. Pounce the center.

Pull petals from center, using a #12 flat brush with School Bus Yellow.

GENERAL INFORMATION

Practice Painting

The old saying is true, "Practice makes perfect." The best way to master the One Stroke technique is to practice painting your strokes directly on top of my strokes. The worksheets in this book are the actual sizes that I have painted them so that when you use the brushes as instructed, your strokes will be the same size as those shown on the Worksheets. There are two ways to practice your strokes.

Using Worksheets in Books

Open book to the Worksheet with the design you wish to practice. Place a piece of acetate or stiff clear plastic directly on top of the worksheet page. Tape it in place so that it won't move.

Paint your strokes directly on the plastic, mimicking my strokes. With practice, your strokes will look just like mine.

Reusable Teaching Guides

There is a wide selection of plastic laminate One-Stroke Teaching Guides to aid in your practice.

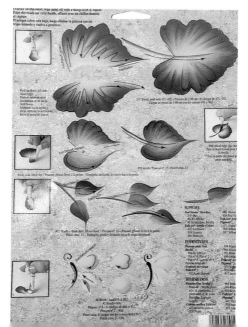

Load the size brush as indicated and paint directly on the teaching guide. Simply wipe off your practice strokes and use them again and again until you are pleased with your progress.

Patterns

Place tracing paper over the pattern you wish to transfer. Neatly trace the design with a pencil.

Position tracing on surface, then slip a piece of transfer paper under tracing. Retrace the design. Hint: you can use a different color pencil or pen for your second tracing so that you can see if you have traced all the lines.

Remove tracing and transfer paper to reveal the transferred design.

Painting on Wood, Papier Mache & Other Porous Surfaces

PAINT TO USE

FolkArt® Acrylic Colors and **FolkArt Artists' Pigments**™ are great for painting on all kinds of porous surfaces, including wood, papier mache, and paper. They dry to a matte sheen. Because FolkArt® paints are acrylic-based, cleanup is easy with soap and water.

SURFACE PREPARATION

Wood: Sand with sandpaper to smooth. Wipe away dust with a tack cloth. Prime raw wood with primer, let dry, and sand smooth before basecoating. Wood can also be prepared with **FolkArt® Sanding Sealer**. See page 12 for more information.

Papier mache and paper: Be sure the surface is free of dust, and you're ready to paint!

FINISHING

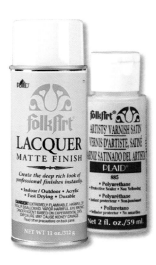

Spray-on **FolkArt® Lacquers** are my favorites for final finishing. They provide good protection from weather and sun, are non-yellowing, and convenient and easy to use. They come in three finishes: Matte, Satin, and Gloss.

FolkArt® Waterbase Artists' Varnish is a brush-on finish that creates a clear satin sheen.

Painting on Glass, Ceramics & Tile

With FolkArt Enamels, you can achieve a durable, opaque, glossy sheen with the one-step painting technique. No primer or finish is needed.

PAINT TO USE

FolkArt Enamels are easy to use paints specially formulated for use on glass and glazed ceramics. They are highly pigmented for excellent coverage, and are water-based and non-toxic. The paints can be mixed and blended. When dried and cured, the paint is top-shelf dishwasher safe.

DIRECTIONS FOR USE

1. Wipe the glass or glazed ceramic surface with rubbing alcohol.

2. Shake paints before applying and paint your design.

3. Allow paints to air dry 21 days before using OR bake. To bake, let paint dry one hour; then place the project in a cool oven. (**Do not** preheat!) Heat the oven to 350 degrees and bake the project for 30 minutes. Allow oven to cool with project in it. When completely cool, remove from oven.

Consideration: If the glass item is hand blown and has bubbles or if there are parts that are glued together, you may not want to bake it. The glued parts may come apart in the heat; handblown items may be damaged by heat. *Tip:* If baking, test bake one item if you are making a large batch or before you spend a long time painting.

A holiday-themed glass plate is painted with FolkArt® Enamels™.

Painting on Glass

Because food should not come in contact with surfaces painted with FolkArt
Enamels, I like to do a reverse painting technique on glassware. I paint
on the backs of clear glass plates so I can use them for serving or eating.
With the reverse painting technique, you paint the foreground items first;
in other words, paint from the front of the design to the back.

REVERSE PAINTING TECHNIQUE

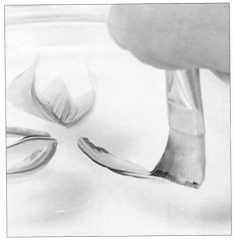

1. The calyxes of the roses are painted first.

2. The leaves are added.

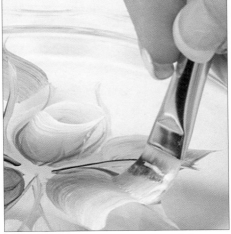

3. Paint the bottom sections of the rosebuds. (Usually, the bottoms are painted after the tops.)

4. Then the tops of the rosebuds are added. Notice one of the rosebuds on this plate has been painted the wrong way.

5. After the design is painted, I dab on a background using the scruffy brush. This gives the design a solid background and allows the beautiful rosebuds to show up better.

The design on this glass plate was painted on the back of the plate using the reverse painting technique.

115

Painting on Glass

USING CLEAR MEDIUM

Clear Medium (4035) thins FolkArt® Enamels to create a more transparent painted design. I like to use Clear Medium when I paint shadow leaves (leaves in the background). The rest of the design is painted first, then the shadow leaves are added to fill in and give depth to the design.

1. After painting the foreground leaves in the design, work brush back and forth on your palette to remove the excess paint. Do not wash the brush – you want a dirty brush to paint the shadow leaves.

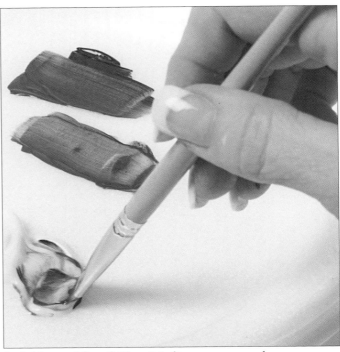

2. Add a puddle of Clear Medium to your palette. Load the brush with Clear Medium by pulling Clear Medium from the edge of the puddle into the brush.

3. Paint the leaves. See how they look very light and transparent.

tips

Curlicues are a breeze to make using Clear Medium. Mix the medium 1-1 with water. Use this mixture to dilute the Enamels paint to an inky consistency. To paint curlicues, use the #2 script liner with the diluted paint.

You can create transparent painted effects on glass using FolkArt® Clear Medium with FolkArt Enamels™.

SHADOW LEAVES WORKSHEET

(A) Shadow leaves painted with Clear Medium and Thicket

(B) Shadow leaves painted with Clear Medium, Thicket, and Dioxazine Purple

(C) Shadow leaves painted with Clear Medium + a touch of Dioxazine Purple

With FolkArt® Enamels™, it's easy to paint on glass surfaces. And the designs will last and last — you can even wash them on the top shelf of your dishwasher!

119

Painting on Metal

FolkArt® Enamels™ work well on metal surfaces, too.

PAINT TO USE

FolkArt® Enamels™ are also great on metal surfaces. They are highly pigmented and possess exceptional hide and superior scratch resistance. And they're waterbase and certified non-toxic.

SURFACE PREPARATION

Painted or enameled metal requires only damp sponging with water and drying – then you're ready to paint.

Galvanized tin has an oily film that must be removed before painting. To wipe it clean, use a sponge or cloth and a solution of two parts water and two parts vinegar. Don't immerse the piece in water (the water can become trapped in areas of the piece and can cause problems later). Dry the piece thoroughly before painting.

Painting on Fabric

The One Stroke technique can be used on fabric with great
success. Mixing Textile Medium with FolkArt paint
helps the paint glide over the surface.

PAINT TO USE

Use **FolkArt® Acrylic Colors** or
FolkArt Artists' Pigments™ mixed
with **FolkArt Textile Medium** for permanent, washable painted effects on
fabrics.

tips

• **Surface Preparation:**

Wash and dry the garment or fabric item according to the manufacturer's
instructions before painting. This will remove sizing and excess dye and mini-
mize shrinkage later on. Do not use fabric softener. Iron the fabric so it's smooth.

When you're ready to paint, use a cardboard shirtboard under the area you
are painting. (You can buy a shirtboard or make one by covering a piece of
cardboard with plastic wrap.)

• **Mixing the Medium**

One your palette, mix one part Textile Medium with two parts of each
FolkArt paint color you will be using. Using the Medium will help paint to
flow better for application and it allows it to become wash-safe.

• **Curing**

Let the painted garment or fabric dry for 24 hours, then heat set by placing
a pressing cloth over the painted design and ironing for 30 seconds over the
pressing cloth at the highest heat setting appropriate for the fabric.

Painting a Pansy on Fabric

1. The back panel is painted first.

2. The two side petals are added.

3. The front petals are painted next.

FolkArt® Textile Medium was mixed with FolkArt® Acrylic Colors before painting the design on this pillow.

Painting on Plastic

PAINT TO USE

Plaid's **Paint For Plastic**™, when dry, is permanent on plastic surfaces; it won't chip off like conventional acrylics. Its smooth, opaque finish is perfect for decorative uses. Easy to use and quick-drying, Paint For Plastic is water-resistant – so it's great for outdoor as well as indoor projects.

Paint For Plastic can be used with One Stroke brushes and with other painting tools, such as sponges and stencils.

tips

- The only preparation needed is cleaning. Clean the item with rubbing alcohol. In all cases, let the item dry thoroughly before painting. Otherwise, there could be places where the paint will not adhere or will slide.

- On flexible surfaces, undercoat your painting with **Paint for Plastic Primer** (1396). It makes Paint for Plastic adhere to bendable plastic surfaces.

- Use **Paint for Plastic Sealer** (1398) to seal and protect painted surfaces for added durability on frequently used or outdoor projects.

124

Sunflower painted with
FolkArt® Enamels

INDEX